An Interdisciplinary Approach to Early Childhood Education and Care

An Interdisciplinary Approach to Early Childhood Education and Care explores early childhood education and care in Australia from a variety of perspectives, highlighting the complexity of working within the field and the need for a truly interdisciplinary approach. It argues that only a holistic understanding of each perspective will allow a clear future for early childhood education within Australia, and that all government parties should provide better outcomes around policy and provision to ensure the support and development of the sector.

Chapters offer insights into how children and families are positioned in educational reform by examining current government policy, as well as individual and collective initiatives. Key paradigms considered include positivist, behavioural, developmental, economic, sociocultural and postmodern models. Garvis and Manning identify challenges to the field and propose improvements needed to develop an interdisciplinary approach to help close the disadvantage gap on educational outcomes. With recommendations aimed at stakeholders within different disciplines, it is hoped that this book will encourage significant improvements to early childhood education and care within Australia.

Providing important insights into the landscape of early childhood education and care, this book promotes new ways of thinking of policy and provision development for the future. As such, it will be of interest to researchers, academics and postgraduate students in the fields of early years education, education policy and politics, and sociology of education, as well as those studying childcare alongside economics, criminology and sociology.

Susanne Garvis is Professor of Child and Youth Studies at the University of Gothenburg, Sweden.

Matthew Manning is Associate Professor in the ANU Centre for Social Research and Methods, Australian National University, Australia.

Routledge Research in Early Childhood Education

This series provides a platform for researchers to present their latest research and discuss key issues in Early Childhood Education.

Books in the series include:

Children as Citizens
Engaging with the child's voice in educational settings
Pauline Harris and Harry Manatakis

Early Years Second Language Education
International perspectives on theory and practice
Edited by Sandie Mourão and Mónica Lourenço

iPads in the Early Years
Developing literacy and creativity
Michael Dezuanni, Karen Dooley, Sandra Gattenhof and Linda Knight

Teaching for Active Citizenship
Research insights from the fields of teaching moral values and personal epistemology in early years classrooms
Joanne Lunn Brownlee, Susan Walker, Eva Johansson and Laura Scholes

Early Childhood Education Management
Insights from practice
Mary Moloney and Jan Pettersen

Early Childhood Education for Muslim Children
Rationales and practices in South Africa
Hasina Banu Ebrahim

An Interdisciplinary Approach to Early Childhood Education and Care
Perspectives from Australia
Susanne Garvis and Matthew Manning

An Interdisciplinary Approach to Early Childhood Education and Care

Perspectives from Australia

Susanne Garvis and
Matthew Manning

LONDON AND NEW YORK

First published 2017
by Routledge
2 Park Square, Milton Park, Abingdon, Oxon OX14 4RN

by Routledge
711 Third Avenue, New York, NY 10017

Routledge is an imprint of the Taylor & Francis Group, an informa business

© 2017 Susanne Garvis and Matthew Manning

The right of Susanne Garvis and Matthew Manning to be identified as authors of this work has been asserted by them in accordance with sections 77 and 78 of the Copyright, Designs and Patents Act 1988.

All rights reserved. No part of this book may be reprinted or reproduced or utilised in any form or by any electronic, mechanical, or other means, now known or hereafter invented, including photocopying and recording, or in any information storage or retrieval system, without permission in writing from the publishers.

Trademark notice: Product or corporate names may be trademarks or registered trademarks, and are used only for identification and explanation without intent to infringe.

British Library Cataloguing-in-Publication Data
A catalogue record for this book is available from the British Library

Library of Congress Cataloging-in-Publication Data
Names: Garvis, Susanne, author. | Manning, Matthew, author.
Title: An interdisciplinary approach to early childhood education and care : perspectives from Australia / Susanne Garvis and Matthew Manning.
Description: Abingdon, Oxon ; New York, NY : Routledge is an imprint of the Taylor & Francis Group, an Informa Business, [2017]
Identifiers: LCCN 2016037537 | ISBN 9781138943391 (hbk) | ISBN 9781315672489 (ebk)
Subjects: LCSH: Early childhood education—Australia. | Interdisciplinary approach in education—Australia. | Educational equalization—Australia.
Classification: LCC LB1139.3.A8 G37 2017 | DDC 372.21—dc23
LC record available at https://lccn.loc.gov/2016037537

ISBN: 978-1-138-94339-1 (hbk)
ISBN: 978-1-315-67248-9 (ebk)

Typeset in Galliard
by Apex CoVantage, LLC

Contents

List of figures		vi
List of tables		vii
Abbreviations		viii

1   Australia and early childhood education and care   1

2   Policy perspectives in Australia   11

3   Education perspectives in Australia   38

4   Economics perspectives in Australia   62

5   Developmental lifecourse theory perspectives in Australia   87

6   Closing the educational gap between mainstream and Indigenous children   119

7   Where to next for early childhood education and care? The importance of an interdisciplinary approach   141

    Index   152

Figures

3.1	Educational Change Model for Early Childhood Education (Garvis et al., 2013, p. 87)	52
3.2	Typical Pattern of Educational Change (Garvis et al., 2013, p. 87)	53
3.3	Fast-Tracked Pattern of Educational Change (Garvis et al., 2013, p. 88)	54
5.1	Model of Program Influences on Conduct Disorder and Antisocial Behaviour. Adapted from Olds et al. (1999)	92
5.2	Trends in Rates of Mortality (All-Cause) from 1900 to 2000	96
5.3	Trends in Life Expectancy for Males and Females Aged One Year (1900–2000)	96
5.4	Trends in Life Expectancy for Males and Females Aged 30 Years (1900–2000)	97
5.5	Bronfenbrenner's Ecological Framework for Human Development	98
5.6	Weighted Average Effect Sizes (d) Corrected for Sample Size. Source: Manning, Homel and Smith (2010)	109
6.1	Percentage of 0–5-Year-Olds in ECEC Services in Australia. Data derived from O'Conner et al. (2016)	122
6.2	The Effect of ECEC Attendance on Behavioural Outcomes. Adapted from Biddle and Arcos Holzinger (2015)	131
6.3	The Effect of ECEC on Reading and Literacy Proficiency. Adapted from Biddle and Arcos Holzinger (2015)	132
6.4	The Effect of ECEC on Maths Ability and Abstract Reasoning. Adapted from Biddle and Arcos Holzinger (2015)	133

Tables

2.1	Educational Program and Practice	20
2.2	An ECEC System to Aim For. Source: Childcare and Early Childhood Learning: Overview, Inquiry Report No 73, Canberra	29
3.1	Content within Early Childhood Teacher Education Programs	46
4.1	The Benefits of Early Childhood Education and Skills Development. Adapted from Karoly, Kilburn and Cannon (2005)	64
4.2	Economic Benefits of Selected Early Childhood Education and Skills Development Programs	66
4.3	Health Effects of the Carolina Abecedarian Project (Age 35). Adapted from Campbell et al. (2014)	70
4.4	Treatment Effect on Average Log Earnings at Age 22. Adapted from Gertler et al. (2014b)	73
4.5	Selected Estimates of Internal Rates of Return (%) and Benefit-to-Cost Ratios. Adapted from Heckman et al. (2010)	77
4.6	Ten Largest Philanthropic Foundations in Australia, 2010–11	79
5.1	Life Expectancy at Birth around 1910 and in 1998. Adapted from The World Health Organisation (1999)	95
5.2	Outcome Domains and Operationalisations. Source: Manning, Homel and Smith (2010)	103
5.3	Programs Included in the Manning et al. (2010) Study. Source: Manning, Homel and Smith (2010)	104
6.1	AECD Domains and Sub-Domains. Source: Goldfeld et al. (2015)	126
6.2	Cognitive and Non-Cognitive Outcome Measures Used by Biddle and Arcos Holzinger (2015). Source: Biddle and Arcos Holzinger (2015)	130

Abbreviations

ABS	Australian Bureau of Statistics
ACECQA	Australian Children's Education and Care Quality Authority
AECD	Australian Early Development Census Domains
ARACY	Australian Research Alliance for Children and Youth
AIHW	Australian Institute for Health and Welfare
COAG	Council of Australian Governments
DEEWR	Department of Education, Employment and Workplace Relations
DLC	Developmental Lifecourse Theory Perspective
ECEC	Early Childhood Education and Care
LSIC	The Longitudinal Study of Indigenous Children
OECD	Organisation for Economic Co-operation and Development

Chapter 1

Australia and early childhood education and care

Early childhood education and care in Australia is a growing field, with more demand from families than ever. Over the last decade there have been many changes within the early childhood sector, including greater government intervention and changes in policy provision. What is unclear, however, is the future of early childhood education and care in Australia and what this means for young children and their families. This chapter will provide a snapshot of the past in regards to early childhood education and care, before providing a quick snapshot of the present landscape. It will then introduce the different perspectives around early childhood education that you will discover in the book. Our stance as researchers will also be shared. The hope of the book is to inform people more about the landscape of early childhood education and care and to promote new ways of thinking of policy and provision development for the future.

Introduction

Early childhood education and care within Australia has had significant reform in the past years. It has become a highly politicized issue around issues of quality, affordability and accessibility. In each election, policies within early childhood education and care are hotly debated and scrutinized.

Within the history of early childhood education and care, the terms of *education* and *care* have often been split. Both education and care services types were provided and delivered by separate organizations and delivered in different locations (Spirit, 1974). When state governments become involved, preschool (the year before formal schooling) was associated with education departments, while provision for younger children was assumed under the responsibility of care and within social services. Over time, preschool has been associated with education and learning, while childcare has not been given the same respect as recognition.

Throughout the 1970s and 1980s, parallel systems of *education* and *care* developed across Australia (Brennan, 1998). In the late 1980s, the privatization of the early childhood sector continued with lobbying by private providers to amend the *Child Care Act* to allow subsidies to be paid to users of for-profit as well as non-profit childcare centers.

In 1996, the election of the Howard government intensified the marketization of care, removing the small subsidies paid to non-profit services. This suggested that the government allowed and supported the privatization of the early childhood sector. Today the majority of the early childhood sector in Australia is within the private sector. The sector continues to grow as more demand is sought from families of young children.

This brief introduction shows the complexity of the Australian early childhood education and care sector. The approach taken by the government has been different to many other countries around the world, with many countries choosing to have government ownership and control over early childhood services. The approach taken by the Australian government has been described by Sumsion (2012) as a national experiment in corporatized early childhood education and care.

The focus of this chapter is to provide a short summary of the current situation of Australian early childhood education and care, before providing a summary of each of the proceeding chapters. Each proceeding chapter describes different perspectives within the Australian early childhood education and care sector. The authors' stance is also disclosed in a type of reflexive statement, allowing the reader to understand the position and reasoning of the two authors. Their stance also includes a call for a greater focus on interdisciplinary ways of working within early childhood education and care as a step forward. Both authors acknowledge that interdisciplinary ways of working provides new possibilities and hopes for the challenges faced within the Australian early childhood education and care sector.

In the context of this book, *early childhood education and care* also includes the concepts of *early childhood development* and *early childhood*. The term is also used to describe other terms used within Australia such as *childcare, early learning* and *early childhood*. While each of the terms has a different definition, in the concept of this book they are considered under a bigger umbrella term of *early childhood education and care*.

A brief snapshot of early childhood education and care in Australia

The benefits of high-quality early education and care

Over the past decade and a half, a rapid growth in early childhood education and care provision has occurred around the world. Simultaneously, there has been greater attention by governments to invest in the years before compulsory schooling, prompted by research highlighting that increased spending in the before-school sector reduces short- and long-term costs to society and promotes the development of better education, health and socio-economic stability (Heckman, 2006). Specifically, Heckman argues:

> *Investing in disadvantaged young children is a rare public policy initiative that promotes fairness and social justice and at the same time promotes productivity in the economy and in society at large. Early interventions [including*

education] targeted toward disadvantaged children have much higher returns than later interventions such as reduced pupil-teacher ratios, public job training, convict rehabilitation programs, tuition subsidies, or expenditure on police. At current levels of resources, society overinvests in remedial skill investments at later ages and underinvests in the early years

(p. 1902).

The collapse of ABC learning centers

In 1988, Eddy Groves and his wife opened a childcare centre in Brisbane, followed by successful ownership of other centres. Run as a franchise model, the centres quickly expanded across Australia and were listed on the Australian stock exchange, becoming the dominant player in Australian long day care (Ellis, 2009). At its peak, the Australian company was worth $2.5 billion (AUD), making Eddy Groves one of the richest people at the time under 40, with his personal wealth estimated at $272 million (AUD) (Baroque, 2006). Other companies quickly followed and within a few years Australia had experience a shift towards corporate care that was provided by companies whose shares were traded on the stock exchange (Sums ion, 2012). However in 2007 the share price fell rapidly, with the company having to go into administrative receivership after fallout from a subprime mortgage crisis. The company went into voluntary liquidation in 2008, creating chaos for Australian families who attended one of the 1,200 centres. At this time it had 25 per cent of centre-based long day care services in Australia, with 120,000 children and 16,000 staff (Ellis, 2009). Fifty-five ABC centres were closed immediately and the government paid $24 million (AUD) to keep the remainder open.

The ABC network was eventually sold in December 2009. Most centres (650) were sold to a coalition of charitable organisations (The Benevolent Society, Mission Australia, the Brotherhood of St Laurence and Social Venture Australia) that created a non-for-profit group known as Good Start.

The ABC network was subject to much criticism and controversy. The Community Child Care Co-Operative in New South Wales argued that the profits of ABC Learning were created from inequitable low staff wages and cost-cutting, both linked to the quality of early childhood education and care. The group also argued that the business model of early childhood education was not sustainable (Djokovic, 2002). Other concerns included the expansion of the company to create a monopoly on childcare services. The Australian Competition and Consumer Commission reviewed the company's operations and imposed certain conditions such as closing centres in some areas and agreeing not to purchase in others (Australian Competition and Consumer Commission, 2004).

Australia's push to improve the early educational sector

In light of the demonstrated benefits to individuals and society at large of providing high-quality education and care and in the early years (c.f. Manning, 2008;

4 Australia and early childhood education and care

Manning, Homel & Smith 2010), Australia has undergone policy transformations with the goal of becoming one of the world's leaders in this area. The strong focus on early childhood in Australia was initiated in 2007, when the Commonwealth Government responded with a higher-level commitment to improve the quality and provision of early childhood education and care. A key initiative was the endorsement of the *National Early Childhood Development Strategy – Investing in the Early Years* in 2009 by the Council of Australian Governments (COAG). The Strategy is a " . . . collaborative effort between the Commonwealth and the state and territory governments to ensure that by 2020 all children have the best start in life to create a better future for themselves and for the nation" (COAG, 2009). The Strategy proposed six priority areas for change:

1   Strengthening universal maternal, child and family health services;
2   Providing support for vulnerable children;
3   Engaging parents and the community in understanding the importance of early childhood development;
4   Improving early childhood infrastructure;
5   Strengthening the workforce across ECD and family support services; and
6   Building better information and a solid evidence base.

The Council of Australian Governments also agreed to a *National Quality Framework for Early Childhood Education and Care* in 2010, which established a National Quality Standard from 2012 to ensure high-quality education and care is consistent across all states and territories (COAG, 2009). The Australian Government (2013) recognizes that early childhood is not only a predictor of the child in Australia today; it is also a predictor of future health and human capital.

Currently, more than 900,000 children attend early childhood services in Australia (Australian Bureau of Statistics, 2015). Within Australia, childcare and early learning is provided with a market services model, often within the private sector (71 per cent) (Commonwealth of Australia, 2011). Only 3 per cent of services are government-managed centers, with the remaining falling under community management (26 per cent). While improvements have been made, there are still significant gaps of concern that require immediate attention. These include (McKenzie, Glover, & Ross, 2014, p. 5):

- Thirty-two per cent of children living in the most socio-economically disadvantaged Australian communities are developmentally vulnerable on one or more of the Australian Early Development Index (AEDI) domains (Centre for Community Child Health and Telethon Institute for Child Health Research, 2009).
- Some 17.5 per cent of these children are developmentally vulnerable on two or more of the AEDI domains (Centre for Community Child Health and Telethon Institute for Child Health Research, 2009).
- The proportion of children enrolled in preschool in the year before full-time school is lower for children from low socio-economic backgrounds.

- The National Quality Standards have revealed that low socio-economic status and remote students have a lower quality of care in early childhood than the average (ACECQA, 2013).

Other concerns are also Australia's performance in the OECD indicators, with Australia ranked in the bottom third. Australia is also ranked 30 out of 34 OECD countries for the percentage of children attending preschool (ARACY, 2013). Other areas of concern within OECD indicators are the number of jobless families, infant mortality, incidences of diabetes and asthma, young children accessing education and young children's exposure to carbon dioxide emissions (ARACY, 2013). Another major concern has been the number of children on care and protection orders, which has doubled in the past decade (AIHW, 2012).

Although Australia has made advances with respect to advancing the sector via the new National Quality Framework, there is a long way still to go before the Australian Government realizes its goal of becoming a world leader in the provision of early childhood education and care. Achieving such a goal cannot occur in the absence of interdisciplinary research highlighting where and how Australia makes changes to support both educators and children.

While clearly much effort has been placed on researching early childhood education and care in Australia by various academic disciplines (e.g. education, development and economics), often, different disciplines attempt to advance the knowledge base from different perspectives and often in a fragmented way (i.e. non-integrative approach). In addition, this knowledge is often published in areas specific to the discipline (i.e. discipline-specific journals). The above issues make it extremely difficult for policy makers to access and consolidate this important evidence. Thus, disciplinary silos and issues relating to information access and fragmentation can moderate the development of effective policy.

Positioning Australia within the international context

Many countries, like Australia, are dedicated to improving the provision of early childhood education and care for children and their families. Many developed countries have a shared focus of providing universal access, learning programs, access and affordability. How this is implemented, however, across various countries, depends on the roles of governments and the positioning of early childhood education and care as a private or public good. In some countries, early childhood education and care policies are part of an overall family policy, allowing parents to work to decrease child poverty. To achieve such a goal, some governments may provide cheap early childhood education and care.

Many countries also experience the problems associated with disciplinary silos and the related fragmentation of child and family services. While this book focuses mainly on the Australian context, many parallels can be drawn with the international sector. Lessons can be learned from the Australian context around policy and practice. The Australian early childhood education and care system can

6 Australia and early childhood education and care

be considered similar to some countries, but largely different to others. Readers can begin to position Australia within the larger global context of early childhood education and care and find positive and challenging examples of policy and practice. By reflecting on a country's context, the reader is also challenged to compare and contrast with other countries they may know about or have experienced around early childhood education and care.

The different perspectives within the book

The book is intended to provide an overview of the different perspectives that are encompassed within Australian early childhood education and care. These perspectives sometimes align and diverge with their aims and outcomes in regards to children and their families. The perspectives are also based within research disciplines, with historical understandings of culture and context embedded within traditions of research and practice.

This book is innovative as it is one of the first books to explore Australian early childhood education and care from a variety of perspectives, arguing for a multidisciplinary approach. The aim of this book is, therefore, to provide: (1) an understanding regarding the complexity of working within the Australian early childhood education and care sector; (2) a summary of the challenges the sector faces; and (3) different perspectives on how the sector can move forward to address these challenges. In short, this book will review and evaluate:

1 Current government policy that shapes the future of early childhood education and care in Australia;
2 Challenges to the early childhood education and care sector identified in the education literature;
3 Challenges to the early childhood education and care sector identified in the economics literature;
4 Challenges to the early childhood education and care sector identified in the literature; and
5 Closing the gap in outcomes for diverse populations.

Each perspective offers the reader insight into how that discipline envisages the positioning of children and families in educational reform, as well as how they view individual versus collective initiatives. Key paradigms to be explored include positivist, behavioral, maturational, developmental, socio-cultural, cultural-historical, postmodern and poststructural. In short, this book will report findings on the current perspectives held by the various disciplines regarding early education policy development in Australia. The final chapter brings each of the disciplines together, arguing for a more multidisciplinary perspective as the way forward for the future of early childhood education and care provision in Australia. The book will also make a case to collective agencies and individuals about overcoming the shortcomings in current early childhood system through an effective early childhood program that allows all young children to develop their capacities to be effective members of society. Each of the perspectives is discussed below.

The first perspective introduced in the book is policy within the second chapter. The political perspective encompasses all policies and provisions provided by the Australian government. This includes provision for parental leave, the availability and affordability of early childhood education and care, policies around the education requirements for young children. Other policy provisions also include teacher education, staff requirements and the assessment and evaluation of quality within early childhood education settings. In the last section of the second chapter, Australian policy is compared to Sweden and Poland. This provides a short overview of how Australian policy compares to other countries. The chapter also concludes with key recommendations for the government to consider in regards to future improvement within Australian early childhood education and care policy.

The next chapter (Chapter 3) provides a summary of the current education perspective within Australia and provides detail and explanation about the proposed learning programs. This allows the reader to see the intended outcomes of learning within current Australian early childhood education. Teacher qualifications are also explored in detail including the government agency tasked with overseeing teacher qualifications across Australia. Current challenges are also identified within the education perspective to show the complexity of the current context. The final section within Chapter 3 also compares the policy and provision of early childhood education with Hong Kong early childhood education provision. Hong Kong is considered one of the most competitive education systems in the world. Comparisons provide possibilities for reflecting on the current Australian system of early childhood education and care.

Chapter 4 introduces early years educators, academics, students and practitioners to the economics perspectives around early childhood education and skills development. The chapter has a particular focus on how investments in early childhood education and care can improve health outcomes, boost future earnings and lead to a strengthened economy. Key trends in Australian early childhood education and care services are explored, including a focus on children and their families. The argument about adequate evidence from policy is also put forward, alongside a discussion on long-term investment in human capital and development.

The developmental lifecourse theory perspective (DLC) in Australia is presented in Chapter 5. The focus of the chapter is to examine DLC evidence, making distinctions between developmental prevention and early intervention. The chapter also introduces readers to the important barriers to knowledge about DLC and how these can be overcome using traditional scientific methods.

The sixth chapter explores the state of Indigenous early childhood education and care in Australia. By examining the problems, it also shows potential solutions using a combination of perspectives discussed in the earlier chapters. Questions are explored about whether education has the strength to overcome the vicious cycle that Aboriginal people face in rural and remote areas.

8 Australia and early childhood education and care

The final chapter (Chapter 7) introduces an interdisciplinary perspective as a way forward for early childhood education and care in Australia to solve the many problems discussed. This means professionals from the different perspectives work together to provide new meaning and understanding about the challenges within the early childhood sector. While some of the disciplines already work in an interdisciplinary way (for example a doctor, a nurse and a speech therapist), we advocate for a greater focus on interdisciplinary ways of working between policy, education, development and health. By allowing the professionals to work together, each brings their own strengths and complements the skills and knowledge of the other perspectives. It also allows new ways of working to be developed within Australia that will benefit both Australian children and their families. The final chapter also provides a summary of the major areas for consideration within the early childhood education and care sector. This is focused on a reflection on what needs to be improved, as well as considerations for future development and provision to support young children and their families.

Our stance

Our stance within this book is to provide a holistic understanding of each of the perspectives to the reader. Both of us are Australian researchers and have had much to do with the Australian early childhood sector from both a professional research level and a personal level. We are both passionate about improvement within the early childhood sector and realise that the different perspectives need to be acknowledged to allow a clear future for early childhood education within Australia. As part of the future orientation, we also acknowledge the importance of interdisciplinary teams and the opportunities this might offer early childhood education and care. This would include new ways of working that allows the strengths of each profession to be shared. Interdisciplinary ways of working also promote a shared language and understanding about young children and their families, further enhancing the professional work undertaken.

Our stance is also not to state that one government party is better than the other. Rather our intent is to show that all Australian government parties should provide better outcomes around policy and provision for young Australian children and their families. We advocate that changes are needed to ensure the early childhood sector can be supported and developed further over time. This also includes changes in the current positioning of early childhood education within government portfolios as well as better commitments to universal access agreements.

In this book, both authors have been able to combine their views and understanding to share a detailed understanding about the early childhood education context. Coming from different disciplines, they are able to bridge their knowledge and understanding to provide a descriptive understanding of the Australian landscape. The intention of the shared writing is to bridge differences but to also show the gaps in current policy and provision. Both agree that through stronger advocacy, early childhood education and care in Australia can be improved.

Conclusion

This book allows the reader to reflect on the current early childhood system within Australia and realise that while improvements have been made, more work is needed to allow Australia to provide quality early childhood development to all young children and their families. This requires a greater focus on the implementation of policy as well as incorporating interdisciplinary learning across policy and provision in all states and territories. A focus on early childhood education and care also requires a strong commitment by all governments to long-term planning and funding needed to boost the current system. It is only through critical reflection that the real challenges can be identified within the sector, leading to a tipping point of change prompting beneficial and substantial action. We hope that as you read the book, you also start to consider ideas to contribute to such turning points within the early childhood sector.

References

AIHW. (2012). *A picture of Australia's children 2012. Cat. no. PHE 167.* Canberra, Australia: Australian Institute of Health and Welfare.

ARACY. (2013). *Report card: The wellbeing of young Australians.* Canberra, Australia: Australian Research Alliance for Children and Youth (ARACY).

Australian Bureau of Statistics. (2015). *4202.0 – Childhood education and care, Australia, June 2014.* Retrieved 22 October from http://www.abs.gov.au/ausstats/abs@.nsf/mf/4402.0.

Australian Children's Education and Care Quality Authority (2013) *ACECQA Snapshot: A report from the Australian Children's Education and Care Quality Authority.* Canberra, Australia: Australian Children's Education and Care Quality Authority.

Australian Competition and Consumer Commission. (2004). *ACCC note to oppose ANC Peppercorn childcare merger.* Retrieved 27 November 2015 from http://www.accc.gov.au/media-release/accc-not-to-oppose-abc-and-peppercorn-childcare-merger.

Australian Government. (2013). *A snapshot of early childhood development in Australia 2012 — AEDI National Report.* Canberra, Australia: Australian Government.

Brennan, D. (1998). *The politics of Australian child care: Philanthropy to feminism.* Cambridge: Cambridge University Press.

Commonwealth of Australia. (2011). *Early childhood education and care in Australia: A discussion paper prepared for the European Union – Australia policy dialogue, 11–15 April 2011.* Canberra, Australia: Early Childhood Australia.

Council of Australian Governments. (2009). *National partnership on early childhood education.* Canberra, Australia: Australian Government.

Ellis, K. (2009). *Ministerial statement – The future of ABC learning*, 15 September.

Farouque, F. (2006). The other Eddy everywhere, *The Age*, 8 April.

Heckman, J.J. (2006). Skill formation and the economics of investing in disadvantaged children. *Science, 312*, 1900–1902.

Jokovich, E. (2002). *The selling out of children's services.* Retrieved 27 November 2015 from http://www.armedia.net.au/the-selling-out-of-childrens-services.

Manning, M. (2008). *Economic evaluation of the effects of early childhood intervention programs on adolescent outcomes.* (PhD), Griffith University, Brisbane.

Manning, M., Homel, R., & Smith, C. (2010). The impact of early childhood interventions delivered to at-risk populations on non health-related outcomes in adolescence. *Children and Youth Services Review, 32*, 506–519.

McKenzie, F., Glover, S., & Ross, M. (2014). *Australia's early childhood development system: What we know.* Retrieved 27 November 2015 from http://www.australianfutures.org/wp-content/uploads/2014/10/AFP-Early-Childhood-Development-What-We-Know-141212.pdf?COLLCC=2810728575&.

Spearritt, P. (1974). The kindergarten movement: Tradition and change. In D. Edgar (Ed.), *Social change in Australia: Readings in sociology* (pp. 583–596). Melbourne: Cheshire.

Sums ion, J. (2012). ABC learning and Australian early childhood education and care: A retrospective audit of a radical experiment. In E. Lloyd & H. Penn (Eds.), *Childcare markets: Can they deliver an equitable service?* (pp. 209–226). Bristol: The Policy Press.

Chapter 2

Policy perspectives in Australia

In recent years, like many countries, Australia has shown a commitment to improving the quality in early childhood services, arising from the recognised benefits in early years towards life-long outcomes. It is now widely accepted that early childhood education provides sound economic drivers for the wellbeing of a nation, where children in higher-quality early childhood services grow up to be healthier and more productive (Institute for a Competitive Workforce, 2010; Sims, 2013; Walker et al., 2011). However, within the Australian context, early childhood education policy has also been subject to highly politicized intentions, including a continual debate between whether the early childhood care sector is devoted to the 'education of young children' or the 'care of young children'. The initial divide can be seen in the Australian political landscape from the 1900s and continues to this day.

This chapter will provide an overview of early childhood education policy in Australia, including recent changes regarding early childhood provision and parental leave. The chapter will also make comparisons with Sweden, considered a world leader in early childhood education policy and providing strong synergy between parental leave and early childhood provision. Critical reflections will be given at the end of further consideration of early childhood education policy. This also includes a call for commitment from the Australian government to long-term funding and support of early childhood education policy to support young children and their families.

A quick history of early childhood policy in Australia: the education care divide

In order to understand the current early childhood policy context in Australia, we must also have a brief understanding of early childhood services in Australia, including the positioning of others. A historical perspective also provides a deeper understanding of decisions within the Australian policy landscape.

Originally, kindergarten was created in order to educate children and their mothers who came from disadvantaged economic and social backgrounds, where kindergartens were positioned as being able to counteract poverty (Brennan,

12   Policy perspectives in Australia

1994). It was also hoped that by mothers spending time within their kindergarten, they could learn suitable mothering practices. Children would be shaped by the kindergarten curriculum, aimed at teaching the characteristics of future citizens. Kindergartens were therefore seen as a vehicle to allow social reform through education (Robert & Kingston, 2001a). For example, in 1907 it was written by Maybanke Anderson that:

> Every kindergarten is managed by a director, who, with many assistants, tries to lay a foundation for character for the children by training them in habits of truthfulness and courtesy. They help them to love cleanliness and order. They teach them to observe accurately, to express themselves with precision, and by manual training of many kinds they develop deft fingers and a desire for useful work
>
> (Roberts & Kingston, 2001, p. 212).

The intention was to explicitly teach middle-class norms by transmission from middle-class kindergarten teachers (Sims & Hutchins, 2011). Alternatively, childcare services (also known as day nurseries) arose from a welfare context in order to provide childcare for working mothers (Sims & Hutchins, 2011). In such times, mothers would only work if they were sole parents or lived in poverty, where the need for childcare was considered essential to prevent children from living on the streets and becoming a threat to society. Staff working within these early childcare services were not kindergarten-trained, but instead had training in nursery nursing. The focus within childcare services was on physical wellbeing, with appropriate care and hygiene habits (Sims & Waniganayake, 2015).

During this time, childcare services were about women who were trying to seek paid employment because of economic circumstances. The focus was not on the quality of early childhood service provision, but rather the education of mothers, who were not considered 'good'. Quality improvement within these services would not come for decades, when recognition began for the importance of quality of care.

Kindergarten however has had a different history to childcare services. As an early childhood pioneer, Maybanke Anderson argued for suitable training for young kindergarten teachers:

> The young women who do all this need special preparation. It is not light work, and few indeed, if any, are born kindergarteners. Two years of training is necessary, and the Kindergarten Union maintains a college where young women over eighteen are received and prepared to take charge of children, either in home or in a kindergarten
>
> (Roberts & Kingston, 2001, p. 212).

Kindergarten teacher training therefore began in Australia in 1885 beginning with private colleges and the Kindergarten Union of New South Wales.

Examination and certification of kindergarten teachers was taken over by the Teachers' Association in 1903 (Roberts & Kingston, 2001). These events have led to a division between childcare services and kindergarten, even to the present day. Motherhood became associated with childcare, while education became associated with kindergartens, resulting in the significant gaps between the two early childhood services. Nuttall (1992) further suggests that it has contributed to the lack of appreciation of childcare work and the subsequent devaluing of the profession and the role of staff.

The next point of departure is the 1970s. During the 1970s and 1980s, the Australian government focused on early childhood policy that provided opportunities for women to return to work. During the 1990s the Australian government's focus moved more towards affordability. A summary of the evolution of policy assistance in Australia is provided in Box 2.1 below.

Box 2.1 Evolution of Early Childhood Education and Care (ECEC) assistance in Australia

Governments in Australia provide assistance to ECEC through a mix of payments to families, support for providers and the direct provision of services. Historically, the Australian government has funded arrangements for early childhood *care* while state and territory governments have had responsibility for childhood *education*. The Australian government's role in ECEC remains largely confined to funding. State and territory governments provide some funding and are also service regulators and providers. Many local governments also provide specific services in their communities.

Throughout the 1970s and 1980s, the Australian government focused on funding services to increase the number of childcare places for use by women (re)entering the workforce. In the 1990s, the affordability of work-related care became a community-wide issue and the Australian government responded by providing fee assistance directly to families in addition to the assistance already provided to some services. More recently, governments have placed greater emphasis on the role of ECEC in child development and ensuring services are of high quality. Governments have also provided extra financial assistance for ECEC services in rural and remote areas and to developmentally vulnerable children, to improve the equity of access.

Payments to assist families with the cost of ECEC (around $5.7 billion in 2013–14) represent the bulk of Australian government funding for ECEC. The remainder ($1.0 billion in 2013–14) is largely directed to service providers and to quality assurance processes through over 20 separate assistance programs.. All amounts are in Australian dollars (AUD). The three current key assistance measures to families are:

- Child Care Benefit (CCB) is a means-tested benefit targeted towards low- and middle-income families. CCB covers up to 50 hours of ECEC use per child per week (provided parents satisfy an activity test of at least 15 hours per week). The CCB rate is dependent on the number of hours families participate in work-related activities and use of ECEC, the number of children in care and whether they are at or below school age, the type of service (approved or registered) attended and family income. For families that do not satisfy the CCB activity test (including those not working), CCB is available for up to 24 hours of ECEC per week. Grandparent CCB (GCCB) is available for grandparents who are primary carers of children in ECEC services and Special CCB (SCCB) is available for families experiencing financial hardship or for children at risk. GCCB and SCCB meet up to the full cost of ECEC, with no means or activity testing. In 2013–14, CCB expenditure amounted to an estimated $2.9 billion.
- Child Care Rebate (CCR) is a non-means-tested payment that provides additional assistance for families using approved care. CCR provides up to 50 per cent of a family's out-of-pocket childcare costs after any CCB is deducted, up to a maximum of $7,500 per child per year. In 2013–14, CCR expenditure amounted to an estimated $2.7 billion. Around 686,000 families received both CCB and CCR and 89,000 families received only CCB.
- Jobs, Education and Training Child Care Fee Assistance (JETCCFA) provides assistance to eligible parents who qualify for the maximum rate of CCB. It pays most of the gap in out-of-pocket costs not covered by CCB, while a parent is working, studying or training. In 2013–14, JETCCFA expenditure amounted to an estimated $0.1 billion for around 54,000 children (35,000 families).

The Australian government has projected that its expenditure on ECEC will rise from $6.7 billion in 2013–14 to $8.5 billion by 2017–18. State and territory governments have, in recent years, contributed a further $0.8 billion per year in support of ECEC (mainly for preschool programs) and all levels of government offer various concessions and tax exemptions to ECEC providers, particularly to the 34 per cent of providers that are not-for-profit.

Source: Productivity Commission, Childcare and Early Childhood Learning. (2014a). Childcare and Early Childhood Learning: Overview, Inquiry Report No 73, Canberra.

Recent decisions in Australian early childhood policy

Over the past decade and a half, a rapid growth in early childhood education and care provision has occurred in Australia. Simultaneously, there has been greater attention by governments around the world to investing in the years prior to compulsory schooling based on research claims that increased spending in the before-school sector reduces costs to society later in time (OECD, 2006). In 2007, the Commonwealth government responded with a higher-level commitment to improve the quality and provision of early childhood education and care. Prior to 2009, the provision of early childhood education in Australia was the sole responsibility of states and territories. A key initiative was the endorsement of the *National Early Childhood Development Strategy – Investing in the Early Years* in 2009 by the Council of Australian Governments (COAG). The Strategy is explained to be a "collaborative effort between the Commonwealth and the state and territory governments to ensure that by 2020 all children have the best start in life to create a better future for themselves and for the nation" (COAG, 2009a). The Strategy outlines how early childhood services will engage and respond to the needs of children and their families. The Strategy also aimed to link the roles of communities, non-government organizations and all governments (state and national) in shaping children's early childhood development.

The Strategy proposed six priority areas for change to be further developed for COAG in 2010, recognising the different starting points of states and territories and as resources allow (DEEWR, 2011). These strategies are to:

- Strengthen universal maternal, child and family health services;
- Provide support for vulnerable children;
- Engage parents and the community in understanding the importance of early childhood development;
- Improve early childhood infrastructure;
- Strengthen the workforce across Early Childhood Development (ECD) and family support services; and
- Build better information and a solid evidence base.

The Council of Australian Governments also agreed to a *National Quality Framework for Early Childhood Education and Care* in 2010, which established a National Quality Standard from 2012 to ensure high-quality education and care is consistent across all states and territories.

The agreement also included the creation of the first Framework for early childhood called *Belonging, Being and Becoming: The Early Years Learning Framework for Australia* (Department of Education, Employment and Workplace Relations, 2009). The aim of the document was to extend and enrich children's learning from birth to five years, and through to a transition to school. All educators

16   Policy perspectives in Australia

across Australia are expected to engage with the Framework, working towards the five outcomes for children:

1   Children have a strong sense of identity;
2   Children are connected with and contribute to their world;
3   Children have a strong sense of identity;
4   Children are confident and involved learners; and
5   Children are effective communicators.

The Framework may therefore complement, supplement or replace individual state and territory frameworks. *Belonging, Being and Becoming* will be discussed further and reflected upon in Chapter 2, including the celebrations and emerging criticisms of the Framework.

Universal, maternal, child and family health services

The *National Framework for Universal Child and Family Health Services* (Australian Health Ministers Advisory Council, 2009) was created to outline the core services that Australian children and their families should receive. These services would be free (no financial cost), regardless of geographical location and where health care was accessed.

The National Framework was related to other policy and strategic reform areas in relation to the health and development of children. These included:

- The *National Health and Hospital Reform Report*, which addressed the importance of a healthy start to life for children and early intervention.
- The *National Disability Strategy*, to provide a national framework to support people with disability, their families and carers.
- The *National Framework for Protecting Australia's Children, 'Protecting Children is Everyone's Business'*, which emphasised a public health approach to the care and protection of children, young people and their families.

The specific National Framework for Universal Child and Family Health Services focused on children from birth to eight years, with a specific emphasis on additional targets and specialist and intensive services for families with additional needs for children where a health or developmental need had been identified.

The Framework (2009, p. 1) was also designed to deliver a number of benefits including:

- Promoting the availability and the role of universal child and family health services to parents, the community as well as health, education and welfare professionals;
- Promoting consistency of service across jurisdictions;
- Providing a contemporary evidence base for service improvement; and

- Progress towards national performance monitoring and the compilation of national population health data for the purposes of comparison across jurisdictions and subpopulations.

While the Framework was not intended to seek or prescribe service delivery, it was designed to provide suggestions and support for evidence-based practice.

Another initiative has been the Australian Early Development Census, formally known as the Australian Early Development Index, that was designed to provide a snapshot of early childhood development as young children in Australia start their first year of full-time schooling. The Census is completed by teachers during term 2, based on five developmental domains:

1 Physical health and wellbeing
2 Social competence
3 Emotional maturity
4 Language and cognitive skills (school-based)
5 Communication skills and general knowledge

Data was initially collected in 2009, and again in 2012 and 2015. In 2012, around 96 per cent of children participated (Australian Government Department of Education and Training (DET), 2013). The data collected from the Census was intended to help governments and communities understand what policies and practices are working and how support structures could be improved for children and their families. Key findings from the 2012 Census found that 78 per cent of children were developmentally on track, compared to 74 per cent in 2009 (DET, 2013). However it was also found that children who resided in very remote communities in Australia were also likely to be developmentally vulnerable (DET, 2013). Children living in the most economically disadvantaged Australian communities were also more likely to be developmentally vulnerable in each of the Census domains.

National Partnership Agreement on Universal Access to Early Childhood Education

Many developed countries around the world have agreed to provide universal access to high-quality early childhood education. Australia has only recently provided an agreement, allowing all children access. The intention was to raise participation rates in early childhood education.

The Agreement aimed to ensure quality early childhood learning programs are available for all children in the year before full-time schooling. The early learning program was to be delivered by a degree-qualified early childhood teacher for 600 hours a year. The agreement was that:

> The universal access commitment is that by 2013 every child will have access to a preschool program in the 12 months prior to full-time schooling. The preschool program is to be delivered by a four year university qualified early

18 Policy perspectives in Australia

childhood teacher, in accordance with a national early years learning framework, for 15 hours a week, 40 weeks a year. It will be accessible across a National Partnership Agreement on Early Childhood Education diversity of settings, in a form that meets the needs of parents and in a manner that ensures cost does not present a barrier to access. Reasonable transitional arrangements – including potentially beyond 2013 – are needed to implement the commitment to preschool program delivery by four year university qualified early childhood teachers, as agreed in the bilateral agreements.

The Agreement was again endorsed by the Council of Australian Governments during the period from 1 July 2013 to 31 December 2014. The new targets were to include:

- Ninety-five per cent of early childhood education programs to be delivered by a degree-qualified early childhood teacher;
- Ninety-five per cent of children enrolled in the year before full-time schooling, including Indigenous children and children from vulnerable and disadvantaged backgrounds; and
- Ninety per cent attendance rate for children enrolled in early childhood education programs.

According to the Australian Bureau of Statistics (2014), while attendance rates have improved for children across Australia, around 83.2 per cent of children aged four years attended an early childhood program, well below the prescribed targets. On 3 May 2015 a third agreement was entered, with access funded until December.

The provision for universal accesses is provided by states and territories, however funding is federally based. As yet, universal access has not received a firm commitment from the Australian government to become a regular feature of the Australian early childhood education system. Instead it has an uncertain future based on evaluations and reviews of success on a two-year cycle. While many other developed countries in the world have made strong commitments to young children's rights to early childhood education and provided suitable provision, the Australian government still appears to be deciding if funding for early childhood education in the year before schooling is beneficial.

If the focus is to improve children's participation in early childhood settings leading to increases in children health, learning and development, the Australian government should also look to other European countries, which have been able to provide at least two years of free publicly funded early childhood education for all children. Most countries within Europe provide universal access from three years of age, with Sweden, Norway and Slovenia providing access from one year of age (Moss, 2013). In some of the countries, a human rights perspective has also been acknowledged to allow young children to participate in education. For example, the United Nations Convention on the Rights of the Child (1989) recognizes the importance of children having access to participate in education,

Policy perspectives in Australia   19

as well as the opportunity to be heard about decision making. These European countries have made firm commitments to the rights of children and recognise the importance of early childhood education.

Australian Children's Education and Care Quality Authority

The Australian government also established the Australian Children's Education and Care Quality Authority (ACECQA) to create a new national body for early childhood education and care. The Authority was also given the role of creating a new quality standards, an assessment and rating system for the quality standards, early childhood educator qualifications as well as working with regulatory authorities in state and territory governments as they implement the new regulations.

The National Quality Standard (NQS) was designed to set a national benchmark for early childhood education and care services, as well as outside school hours care services in Australia. The National Quality Standard was intended to provide quality improvement through improved educator-to-child ratios, greater individual care and attention for children, educators with increased qualifications, better support for children's learning and development and a national register to help parents assess the quality of education and care services in their area (my.child.gov.au).

Seven quality areas were created, to be assessed within NQS. These were:

1   Educational program and practice
2   Children's health and safety
3   Physical environment
4   Staffing arrangements
5   Relationships with children
6   Collaborative partnerships with families and communities
7   Leadership and service management

Within the seven quality areas there are 18 standards and 58 elements. For example, Table 2.1 demonstrates quality area 1 to show how quality areas, standards and elements fit together (ACECQA, 2013).

Each early childhood service and outside school hour service would receive a rating after a visit from an assessor based on their performance against each of the quality areas, and an overall rating. All rating are published on the government website mychild.gov.au. with details about the early childhood level of quality, fees and vacancies. Services can receive five ratings within the standards and overall (ACECQA, 2013):

•   Excellent rating, awarded by ACECQA
•   Exceeding National Quality Standard
•   Meeting National Quality Standard
•   Working Towards National Quality Standard
•   Significant Improvement Required

20 Policy perspectives in Australia

Table 2.1 Educational Program and Practice

Standard	*Element*
Standard 1.1 An approved learning framework informs the development of a curriculum that enhances each child's learning and development.	Element 1.1.1 Curriculum decision making contributes to each child's learning and development outcomes in relation to their identity, connection with community, wellbeing, confidence as learners and effectiveness as communicators. Element 1.1.2 Each child's current knowledge, ideas, culture, abilities and interests are the foundation of the program. Element 1.1.3 The program, including routines, is organised in ways that maximise opportunities for each child's learning. Element 1.1.4 The documentation about each child's program and progress is available to families. Element 1.1.5 Every child is supported to participate in the program. Element 1.1.6 Each child's agency is promoted, enabling them to make choices and decisions and to influence events and their world.
Standard 1.2 Educators and co-ordinators are focused, active and reflective in designing and delivering the program for each child.	Element 1.2.1 Each child's learning and development is assessed as part of an ongoing cycle of planning, documenting and evaluation. Element 1.2.2 Educators respond to children's ideas and play and use intentional teaching to scaffold and extend each child's learning. Element 1.2.3 Critical reflection on children's learning and development, both as individuals and in groups, is regularly used to implement the program.

Source: ACECQA, 2013

The intention of the MyChild government website follows along similar thinking to primary and secondary school data that is published on the MySchool government website. The intention is to provide transparent accountability, allowing the government to published collected data to the public. It is also hoped to provide families with better information for decisions about attending early childhood services and schools. For example, a parent could make a choice about an early childhood provided based on their assessed quality. Through greater accountability, it is also hoped that parents will also have a level of control over quality by only choosing centers that are currently meeting the national quality standard.

ACECQA is also responsible for helping states and territories meet new required child-to-educator ratios due for implementation on 1 January 2016. The ratios required for centre-based services are:

- Children aged birth to 24 months – one educator to four children
- Children aged 24 months to 36 months – one educator to five children (four children in Victoria)
- Children aged 36 months and up – one educator to 11 children (10 children in New South Wales, Tasmania and Victoria)

While some of these ratios have already been in place, for some locations they are new and require further hiring of staff. In some Australian newspaper reports there have been suggestions that the new staff ratios will lead to increased price hikes in the early childhood sector (e.g. *The Age*, 2 October 2015, "Extra teachers required for kindergartens could hike fees for parents"). Some providers have reported between a 5 per cent to 50 per cent increase in fees, calling for an increase in government funding (Preiss, 2015).

Strengthening the early childhood workforce and family support services

An important area for change in the early years has been raising the standards of qualifications of early childhood educators. This was formalized in the National Quality Framework (2009). The requirements are explicit, and require by 2014 that:

- Half of all staff at every long day care centre or preschool must have (or be working towards) a diploma-level early childhood qualification. The remaining staff will all be required to have (or be working towards) a Certificate III level early childhood education and care qualification.
- An early childhood teacher will be required as part of the staffing establishment in long day care and preschool services for 25 children or more. Additional early childhood teachers will be required for larger services by 2020.
- Family day care coordinators will need to have a diploma level early childhood education and care qualification and family day carers must have (or be working towards) a Certificate III.

The government initiatives were based on research that links higher qualifications of early childhood staff to improved outcomes for children. Early childhood

22 Policy perspectives in Australia

teachers with higher-level qualifications are more likely to engage in appropriate interactions that are sensitive, responsive and engaged (Norris, 2010). This has been linked to greater staff-initiated learning, and staff more engaged in play and social interactions with children (McMullen & Alat, 2002).

ACECQA has also overseen early childhood qualifications. From 1 January 2014, all long day care services and preschool service providing care to less than 25 children were required to have an early childhood teacher for at least 20 per cent of the time. For long day care and preschool services with over 25 children, an early childhood teacher must be attendance for at least six hours a day or 60 per cent of the operating hours. For many services this has meant employing qualified early childhood teachers.

To be assessed as a qualified early childhood teacher, staff can either have their qualifications assessed by ACECQA, or undertake an ACECQA-approved program provided by a training organisation or a university. ACECQA is responsible for approving early childhood teacher qualifications, diploma qualifications, certificate three qualifications and outside school hours care qualifications. Approved providers for first aid, emergency asthma and anaphylaxis requirements are administered by ACECQA. All approved providers are listed on the government website.

Within many of the programs related to working in early childhood services, ACECQA has guidelines for the content and knowledge to be learnt within training and university programs, as well as the number of required professional experience placement days. Training organizations and universities must directly apply to ACECQA to have their qualifications approved. Individuals can also apply to have their qualifications approved. Fees are charged by the government authority to assess applications. In 2014, the fee for approval of early childhood education and care qualifications was AUD$293.

Despite the improvement in teacher qualifications, the requirement to have a qualified early childhood teacher may work as a counter-force to providing all children in long day care with quality education and care. An underlying assumption with current policy reform has been that degree-qualified teachers will work with children under three years of age through a leadership and mentoring role, however government requirements demand that qualified teachers work with preschool-aged children (Rouse, Morrissey, & Rahimi, 2012). Previous research suggests that qualified teachers in childcare centers end up working with older children, while diploma- and certificate-qualified educators (or sometimes unqualified staff) work with the younger children (Ireland, 2006; Norris, 2010; Rouse, 2008). There is also some evidence that pre-service early childhood teachers prefer to work with older children as opposed to younger children (Nolan & Rouse, 2013). This may reflect the low professional status of teachers working in childcare along with salary and other industrial conditions. The professional status of teachers in childcare settings is not comparable to that of teachers in school settings, with a widespread perception that teachers in childcare are not 'real' teachers (Ali, 2009; Sums ion, 2007). Ireland (2006) also notes that there

Funding of early childhood education in Australia

Since 2008, the Australian government has contributed over AUD $2 billion to states and territories as part of National Partnership arrangements (Australian Government Department of Education and Training, 2015). While this may appear significant in terms of funding, Australia still appears to spend less on early childhood education than any other OECD as a proportion of GDP, ranking second last out of all of the OECD countries for which data was available. In 2010, Australia's government expenditure on early childhood education (children aged three years and over) was 0.06 per cent of Gross Domestic Product (GDP), compared to an OECD average of 0.47 per cent of GDP (OECD, 2013). In comparison to other countries around the world that lead early childhood education, Denmark spends over 1 per cent of GDP on early childhood education, Many countries spend over 0.7 per cent of GDP on early childhood education, including Iceland, Spain, Israel, Russia, Luxembourg, Slovenia and France. In many of these countries, 82 per cent of four-year-olds are enrolled in early childhood education across the OECD countries (OECD, 2013).

One of the main differences between Australia and OECD countries, especially in Europe is that the private sector plays a dominant role in early childhood education. The market share of the private sector in Australia is close to 75 per cent. In many OECD countries, early childhood education is a public good, with children attending publicly funded early childhood services. In 2010, private funding accounted for 44 per cent of total expenditure of early childhood education in Australia, compared to an OECD average of 18 per cent (OECD, 2013).

Paid parental leave

Paid parental leave has been a focus in many countries since the 1970s. In 1979, the United Nations suggested:

> In order to prevent discrimination against women on the grounds of marriage or maternity and to ensure their effective right to work, State Parties should take appropriate measures . . . to introduce maternity leave with pay or with comparable social benefits without loss of former employment, seniority, or social allowances.
>
> —United Nations Convention on the Elimination of All Forms of Discrimination Against Women, December 18, 1979

Only two countries today do not have paid parental time off for new parents, Papua New Guinea and the United States. Australia was one of the most recent countries to provide a paid parental leave scheme.

24   Policy perspectives in Australia

In 2011, the Australian government introduced a paid parental leave scheme for a parent (usually the mother). The neighbouring country of New Zealand introduced paid parental leave in 2002. The payment period was for 18 weeks and funded at the Australian minimum wage AUD\$657 before tax). In 2013, the government introduced the dad and partner pay scheme, to allow partners two weeks of minimum wage following the birth or adoption of a child. The maximum however that can be applied for is 18 weeks (either one parent takes all of the 18 weeks, or one parent takes 16 weeks and the other parent takes two weeks). To be eligible, parents required an adjusted taxable income of AUD\$150,000 or less in a financial year. Parents were also required to work 10 months out of 13 months before the birth or adoption, with at least 330 hours in a 10-month period (just over one day a week).

Following the 2013 election, the Liberal Party decided to bring an election promise of increasing paternity leave to six months for parents. This would bring Australia in line with many other OECD countries. Research suggests that at least six months is required for adequate breastfeeding and paternal bonds. Breastfeeding provides numerous health benefits for babies and mothers. It is considered so important for a baby that the World Health Organisation recommends all babies are breastfed until six months of age. As part of their global targets for 2025, the World Health Organisation would like the enactment of six months mandatory paid maternity leave and policies that encourage women to breastfeed in the workplace and in public (UNICEF, 2014).

Numerous research indicates that the longer the maternity leave within a country, the longer the duration of breastfeeding (Guendelman, English, & Chavez., 2009; Kurinij et al., 1989; Mirkovic et al., 2014). Short maternity leave appears to have a negative impact on breastfeeding, especially when, in work for women in non-managerial roles, the work schedule is inflexible and the employee is experiencing psychosocial stress (Guendelman et al., 2009). A recent study has also found that women in the United States who return to full-time work before the infant is three months old are less likely to meet their intentions to breastfeed for at least three months, compared to mothers not working during the first three months (Mirkovic et al., 2014).

The role of the father has also been identified as highly important in early infancy for breastfeeding and has been associated with positive cognitive, developmental and socio-behavioral outcomes (e.g. improved weight in preterm infants, improved breastfeeding rates) (Sarkadi et al., 2008). Greater support is therefore needed for fathers to be involved within breastfeeding.

In 2015, the Australian government decided to make changes to their current paternity leave arrangements, even though six months had been an election promise. This was the introduction of the *Fairer Paid Parental Leave Bill 2015* that stopped working families from claiming both an employer maternity leave scheme and the government paid parental scheme. Many families would apply for both policies to increase the time to care for young infants and engage in breastfeeding, usually 12 weeks from an employer and 18 weeks from the government, bringing a total of just under six months of paid parental leave. The original design of the program was outlined in the Productivity Commission Inquiry Report in 2009 entitled *Paid parental leave: Support for parents with newborn children*. The intention was paid parental leave would co-exist with public and private funding. The report states that it would expect that (2009, p. 7.21):

> many Australian businesses would restructure their existing leave schemes to top up government-funded leave to full replacement wages and then use the balance (if any) to extend the period of leave at full pay.

Women who were drawing on both schemes were publicly declared as 'rorters defrauding the system' by ministers within the media.

The 55 submissions from the bill largely recommended that the new legislation should not be passed. Unions, non-government organizations and academics argued and provided evidence that the scheme was working well, including increasing participation rates for women returning to work. Employer organizations were largely unsupportive of the bill. Despite the overwhelming number of submissions that recommended no change, the government implemented the new legislation, suggesting budget repair was more important than the rights of working mothers within Australia. While other countries around the world might view paternity leave as a working investment allowing mothers to return to work, the Australian government has decided to strip back the scheme. The Human Rights Commission has warned that Australia could be in breach of its international human rights obligations. The Australian Sex Discrimination Commissioner, Elizabeth Broderick, had described the move as retrogressive and inconsistent with international human rights laws as she warned the proposal would "ultimately detract from existing Australian Government policies to improve economic outcomes for women, increase women's workforce participation rates, and reduce the barriers faced by women when balancing work and family responsibilities such as through key initiatives in childcare" (Smerdon, 2015).

The policy change again reflects an Australian government who is uncommitted to long-term early childhood policies to support families and children. It also represents the changing nature of Australian early childhood policy and the way it is influenced by lobby groups and budgetary constraints, completely different to other areas of policy that have always received continued funding and support. What is needed is long-term commitment to the health and welfare of young children and their families, and political decisions that are made on evidence of effectiveness, not three-year political cycles.

Recent decisions from 2014 in Australian policy discussions

In 2014, the Productivity Commission was asked to explore early childhood services within Australia to review early childhood service quality improvement.

While much work had been done to unite education and care within early childhood services during the *National Early Childhood Development Strategy – Investing in the Early Years* in 2009, the Productivity Commission decided to again separate education and care in the title of the report "Child care and early childhood learning". Within the report, there is clear separation between education and care, even for the youngest of children in care. For example, the reports articulates that (2014a, p. 227) "early childhood education and care for children age birth to three should focus on quality of care and not be required to include a significant educational component".

The positioning of the Productivity Commission report appears to also echo a movement internationally that has begun to separate education and care within early childhood services. With a stronger focus on preparedness for school, care appears the dominant pedagogy for children under three, while education becomes the dominant pedagogy for children over three. In order to achieve better outcomes for school preparedness, Ang (2014) argues that

> the pedagogy of supporting children's learning during the early years is becoming increasingly formalised and academics . . . holistic educational experience is somewhat lost in the drive towards targets and attainment, especially when assessment is used as a policy tool in education
>
> (p. 192).

The new focus then provides a different perspective of the role of early childhood education. While it is still seen as a political lever, the focus moves away from providing health and productive future citizens, to a focus on 'schoolification', ignoring the important features early childhood education provides for young children's social and emotional wellbeing, as well as socialisation and recognising that children's development is asynchronous.

The focus on the schoolification also changes a government's perspectives about quality improvement within early childhood services. This is particularly worrying for children aged under three, where an understanding of the theoretical and practical experience expected of qualified teachers may no longer be recognised as needed. The Productivity Commission (2014a) argued that:

> Long day care should be able to provide care for children under 36 months without the oversight of a teacher and these children should not be included in the count towards the requirement to hire an early childhood teacher. This would allow early childhood teachers to focus on children aged 36 months and over. The commission also considers that all long day care workers caring for children aged under 36 months should be required to hold or be actively working towards a certificate III or equivalent (the same qualification expected of family day care educators) rather than half of the educators being required to hold or be working towards a diploma level qualification.

The Productivity Commission report (2014a) appears to fly in the face of evidence-based research about the importance of having bachelor-qualified staff working with the youngest of children. Numerous research studies have shown that to improve young children's learning and development, qualified teachers are needed. In a recent meta-analysis study (studies since 1984) of the relationship between teacher qualifications and the quality of the learning environment within early childhood education, it was found that bachelor-qualified early childhood staff were able to significantly improve the learning quality and the environment for learning (Manning, Garvis, Fleming, & Wong, 2015). The findings provide an important summary to governments interested in evidence to support the up-skilling of staff within early childhood services, not the down-skilling as the Productivity Commission appears to report.

The final report did provide some important statistical facts for the Australian government in regards to parental workforce participation. These included (Productivity Commission, 2014b):

- Some 165,000 parents (on a full-time equivalent basis) would like to work, or work more hours, but are not able to do so because they are experiencing difficulties with the cost of, or access to, suitable childcare (p. 11).
- Australia's tax and transfer system created a strong disincentive for some parents to enter the workforce or to increase their hours of work (p. 11).
- There are long waiting lists for early childhood education and care services in some areas (p. 9).

The report showed that accessibility and affordability were growing concerns within Australia. The report however recommended suggestions that went against current requirements within the National Quality Framework to improve quality. This included the recommendation of deskilling of staff who worked with children aged under three years to working towards a certificate. This implied that children under three years did not require trained staff who would be able to provide educational experiences for the children. Rather the focus was again on 'care', where children under three years needed the least qualified staff working within the early childhood sector. Only qualified early childhood educators were require for children aged three years and over. Recommendations were also made about loosening current ratios and providing greater flexibility with the level of staffing qualifications.

Another highly discussed issue suggested was the incorporation of nannies into the early childhood education and care services profile, allowing subsidies to also extend to the use of nannies. A government trial with nannies will begin in 2016. Questions have been raised about the actual cost of implementing nannies, regulation of nannies and the qualifications of nannies within the Australian landscape. Concerns have also been raised about the potential exploitation of nannies within the early childhood sector, calling for strong regulation and enforcement of control mechanisms. Such concerns are not new

28 Policy perspectives in Australia

with the Australian public. In 2013, Garvis and Pendergast reported the perceptions about nannies of Australian people. The majority of respondents suggested that a nanny was only for a wealthy family and held limited educational qualifications.

The final report provided a system for the Australian early childhood education and care system to aim for. Table 2.2 below (Productivity Commission, 2014b, p. 15) provides the summarized table that governments, providers and families could work towards. The key features "relate to the facilitation of both child development outcomes and parental workforce participation, and the integration of ECEC with other community services and schools" (2014a, p. 15).

Why does early childhood policy continually change ministerial portfolios?

Early childhood policy is related to a number of areas, including social welfare, education, employment and health. The cross-nature of early childhood policy means that in Australia, different governments have prioritised early childhood policy in different ways, at time locating it within different portfolios of social welfare or education.

The placement of early childhood education within government portfolios has also changed numerous times since childcare policies became part of ministerial duties. During the Howard government (1996–2007) childcare services were included in the children and youth portfolios and at times located in family and community services portfolios.

During the first Rudd government (2007) the word *childcare* was actually used in a ministerial portfolio. Originally minister Julia Gillard held the portfolio of education, employment and workplace relations alongside social inclusion. After a cabinet reshuffle, minister Kate Ellis assumed responsibility for early childhood education, childcare and youth.

In 2013, the incoming coalition government positioned childcare within the education portfolio. Another cabinet reshuffle saw childcare and early childhood education and care services transferred to the social services portfolio. As of September 2015, childcare and early childhood education and care services were transferred back to the Department of Education and Training.

The continual changing of positioning provides insights into how governments understand early learning and care. When childcare policies have been placed in Education, there is recognition that childcare policies provide early learning activities for young children and it is part of the educational landscape within Australia. The understanding is that early childhood services are the first institution children encounter for education. Alternatively, when childcare policies are placed within social welfare portfolios, the focus moves to one of care, at the absence of education. It represents childcare policies as primarily a welfare or labour market issue. The continual movement between portfolios creates different perspectives to dominate, with continual changes in related policy.

Policy perspectives in Australia 29

Table 2.2 An ECEC System to Aim For

Children under school age	School-age children
Parents are able to choose from a broad range of ECEC types (including their own care at home) to suit family needs.	All children start school (at an age that is consistently determined across Australia) after completing at least one year of guidance under an early childhood teacher.
A range of non-parental care options available at a range of prices, at least some of which are within most family budgets.	Schools organise appropriate external organisations to provide a range of optional outside school hours (including vacation) care and activities using school and external facilities. Some schools may choose to adjust school hours in order to provide such activities at one rather than both ends of the school day.
ECEC is appropriate quality (consistent with National Quality Standard), age and culturally appropriate and stimulating to child development needs.	
In at least the year before school, children are guided by an early childhood teacher; for those at risk or developmentally vulnerable, this may extend to several years before school age.	These outside school hours care and activity options would be provided at a range of prices, with sufficient places at every school to meet the demand for care of children at that school.
Additional needs children have (at a minimum) access to ECEC on the same basis as other children.	Schools extend care and activity options to cater for onsite preschool students.
ECEC is closely linked in with schools, and family, health and social services.	ECEC services enable all parents to work beyond the hours and weeks of a school year while providing a framework to cope with the juggle of children's development activities outside of school hours.
ECEC services enable all parents to work full or part time with flexibility, as they decide.	
ECEC places not needed on a temporary basis are used by providers for occasional care.	ECEC providers compete to offer a range of quality ECEC services to schools and are able to negotiate contracts that ensure reliability in provision from year to year.
Providers compete to offer a range of quality ECEC services and attract suitable staff.	

Source: Productivity Commission, Childcare and Early Childhood Learning. (2014a). Childcare and Early Childhood Learning: Overview, Inquiry Report No 73, Canberra.

What is needed from the Australian government is a firm commitment to early childhood policy being recognised as early childhood education and care, an essential part of the education system. A permanent place is needed within the

30 Policy perspectives in Australia

portfolio of education and training to acknowledge the important benefits of early learning. It would also provide a smoother transition process for children within educational institutions, with formal recognition that early childhood services are the first provider of education for children. Just as children transition from primary school to high school in Australia, they also can transition from early childhood services to primary school.

Another benefit of having early childhood policy within the education and training portfolio is the alignment of frameworks, curriculum and pedagogy that can be achieved by early childhood services working closely with primary schools. While there is strong alignment between primary school and high school in Australia with curriculum and pedagogy, the same is not true for early childhood services as it has been continually shifted within government ministerial portfolios. For the integration of educational sectors as well as allowing early childhood policy to actually be successfully implemented, the continual movement and fragmentation needs to be acknowledged and addressed within Australian political landscapes. It is only through a permanent home within education that early childhood services can be integrated and implemented to support a child's learning and development.

How does Australian policy differ from leading countries in social policy?

Sweden

While Australia has taken one path with their policy and provision for early childhood policy, it can be compared to other countries that have been ranked as leading in early childhood policy. One of these countries is Sweden, which has allowed the successful reconciliation of work and family life. The aim of the Swedish system is to contribute to improved conditions for good living standards for all families and children, increased freedom of choice and empowerment of parents.

Sweden has a very developed paid parental leave scheme that encourages both parents to spend time with their children. Paid parental leave was introduced in 1974. Together the mother and the father are entitled to up to 16 months of paid leave per child. Close to 90 per cent of fathers also take paid parental leave. Thirteen months are funded by the government at 80 per cent of the parent's wage, with the remaining three months paid at 180 Swedish krona (SEK) per day. Each parent has a non-transferable entitlement of two months, meaning paid parental leave must be shared (currently three months is being discussed in government). Both parents can take 30 days at the same time. To encourage both parents to be involved in caring of the child, a gender equality bonus was introduced in 2008. Parents who both take leave are entitled to the extra bonus. Such a scheme recognizes the importance of shared parenting and allows all parents the opportunity to participate.

In 2012, the employment rate for women was 71.8 per cent, close to men's participation rates in the workforce of 75.6 per cent (European Union, 2014b). The employment rate of mothers of children aged under six is the third highest in the European Union. The gender pay gap in Sweden is also lower than the European Union average (European Union, 2014b).

Respect for parents on parental leave also seems to be strong within Sweden. In a survey conducted by the Swedish Social Insurance Agency looking at employer attitudes to parental leave, only 10 per cent of employers found it problematic that employees were on parental leave, while 70 per cent believed they should motivate employees to share parental leave equally between parents (Försäkringskassan, 2014). The findings highlights that it is important that the "support of social parents and employers is necessary for the successful promotion of parental leave among fathers" (Eurofound, 2015).

In Sweden, around 3.1 per cent of GDP is spent on financial benefits for children and families (European Union, 2014b). The high employment levels of families have led to low child poverty rates among children. In addition to parental benefits, other measures have also been introduced to reduce the financial burden of raising children in Sweden. These include:

- Pregnancy benefits of 80 per cent of a mother's wage for working mothers who are unable to work during pregnancy because of the physically demanding nature of their jobs;
- Child allowance amounting to 1050 SEK per month and per child. Payment will continue until the child reaches 16 years of age.
- Parents are entitled to leave to care for a sick child for 120 days a year for children under 12 years of age. Parents will receive 80 per cent of their wages.

Subsidised childcare is also an important feature of the Swedish system. Parents are guaranteed a place at a preschool (known as förskola) from one year of age, with a maximum cost of 1287 SEK per month. Preschools within Sweden also provide breakfast, lunch and snacks for children. Parental fees can be no more than three per cent of a family's monthly income. The parental fee covers on average, only 11 per cent of the actual cost of a place in preschool, with the rest heavily subsidised by the government. Around 95 per cent of children aged three to six years are enrolled in preschool (European Union, 2014b). Health care (including dental care) and schooling are also free for all children until 18 years of age.

In some Swedish cities, providing access to parents with prams is also important. In Stockholm for example, parents pushing infants and toddlers in prams can ride for free on public buses. This allows parents not to leave their pram unattended while having to pay for transport.

Poland

Another country for comparison is Poland. After a conscious policy effort, Poland has decreased child poverty. To improve the conditions for families and

32 Policy perspectives in Australia

to increase fertility rates, the Polish government is currently implementing a set of supportive family policies to provide sustainable solutions.

In 2013, the Polish government increased paid parental leave from 20 weeks to the possibility of a full year at 80 per cent of salary. Parental leave can be used by both parents at the same time for six months. The intention is to increase women's access to the workforce, to increase from the current level of 53.4 per cent (European Union, 2014a). Mothers are also entitled to special protection against dismissal during parental leave.

The government has also increased Polish expenditure on family and child related benefits to help support families. Tax relief was also increased in 2013 for families with three or more children.

A focus has also been made on increasing children's attendance rates within early childhood services. Around 36 per cent of children between three and school age attend a preschool (European Union, 2014a). Since 2013, the government has reduced charges for children in preschool. Local governments determine the number of hours daily that a child can stay free of charge (minimum five hours per day) and how many additional hours must be paid for by parents if the child stays above the limit. Parents also pay for the meals served to children. In 2014 the government also introduced a school subsidy to help parents purchase textbooks. Health care is also free and children and youth can receive full refunds on drugs.

Another key policy initiative has been the introduction of the Big Family Card in 2014. It is a document that guarantees special rights to families with at least three children, irrespective of income. The policy is designed to provide cheaper public transport, discounts in museums, theatre, national parks as well as helping to support recreational activities. Discounts have been made available to 3.5 million people in Poland (European Union, 2014a).

Critical reflection: what does this mean for Australia?

Australia appears to have a continually moving landscape for early childhood policy compared to other countries. This includes the dichotomy between care and education, regular shifting of the early childhood portfolio within government as well as policies that appear to be focused on short-term rather than long-term funding arrangements. For example, other countries have made firm policies to support paid parental leave and children's access to early childhood educational services, realising the important depth of research related to supporting the wellbeing and development of young children and their families. Other countries also appear to support the return of parents to the workforce after having children, as well as providing assistance with early childhood services. As yet, the policy position and commitment within Australia is unclear.

One of the main reasons for these differences has been the positioning of children and early childhood services within society. In Australia, children are considered a private choice, with early childhood services being a private good. The early childhood sector is dependent on private funding, allowing families to also make private choices about early childhood services. The responsibility for the education, health and development of a child is the responsibility of a parent, who can choose how they would like to fulfil this role.

Alternatively, early childhood services in some countries are considered a public good and heavily funded by the government to support the education, health and development of all children. In such countries, early childhood is also considered a way to decrease child poverty, by allowing all children to have equal access to early childhood services. In such a perspective, parents are provided with early childhood services, however they may not have the same choice as a private market.

The Australian government is now at a crossroad with early childhood policy in regards to commitment and long-term planning. While there is the potential to have a world-class early childhood system that provides support and development for all children and families, decision makers must first realise their own shortfalls in Australian early childhood education policy including:

- Acknowledging the importance of having six months paid parental leave to support the health and development of the child and family. This would allow adequate time for breastfeeding and support child bonds.
- An early childhood system that recognizes that research suggests qualified early childhood staff provide quality learning environments for young children. Rather than the de-skilling of the early childhood profession, they should be supported to increase the level of skills and professionalism.
- Universal access should be given a long-term funding commitment as well as place within Australian legislation. This would demonstrate the Australian government's commitment to the education of young children. Universal access could also be extended down to include children from one or two years of age, acknowledging their right to a quality education.
- The Australian government must read and understand research regarding early childhood education and policy. Many countries have been able to help lead positive policy development and provide models for suitable early childhood systems. As yet the Australian government appears to make limited decisions based on research. Further, the government also appears to not listen to key representatives within the community. For example, the majority of submissions for the paid parental leave review suggested the system was working well and should not be touched. Strong evidence was provided from both the Australian and international context. However none of this evidence appeared to have been drawn upon or even discussed in the final decision. This suggests that political decisions regarding early childhood are not made on evidence, but rather personal opinion and experience.
- Early childhood policy within Australian politics deserves a permanent home within the ministry portfolio of education. Early childhood education has a right to stand alongside primary school education and high school education

in Australia, providing a smooth transition between the sectors within the one educational portfolio. Continual movement is disruptive for the profession and community, suggesting the government is not committed to actually improving the health and wellbeing of young children and their families. No other education groups within government portfolios have had as much movement.

- If the government is committed to reducing the increasing children's poverty rate within Australia, they must look at the success of other early childhood systems around the world. Sweden for example has been able to provide early childhood services that are cheap and provide high-quality education, care and nutrition for young children. All children are guaranteed a place within an early childhood service from one year of age, allowing parents to work. Such a move allows parents to earn money, further decreasing the risk of poverty.
- The Australian government has one of the lowest funding rates for early childhood in the OECD. If the Australian government is committed to the youngest of children and their families within Australian society, they would make firm commitments to higher levels of funding. The funding would allow more children to participate in early childhood services and parents to return to the workforce. While the government has been able to create numerous frameworks, strategies and policies, it has not been able to make a commitment to what is truly needed: higher levels of funding.

Overall this chapter has shown the complex and sometimes confused nature of Australian early childhood policy. It is hoped that decision makers will one day recognise the potential for the Australian early childhood system and make sound decisions based on evidence that can provide strong change within Australian society. Such decisions require visionary politicians who are able to support and invest in the lives of young children and their families. While the Australian government appears committed to supporting children once they are in primary school with access to free education, the same cannot be said for children aged five years and under and their families in Australia.

References

Ali, C. (2009). *Impacts on the professional practice of kindergarten teachers working in long day care.* (Unpublished Honours thesis), Deakin University, Victoria, Australia.

Ang, L. (2014). Preschool or Prep School? Rethinking the Role of Early Years Education. *Contemporary Issues in Early Childhood, 15*(2), 185–199.

Australian Bureau of Statistics. (2014). *Preschool education in Australia 4240.0.* Retrieved 14 October 2015 from http://www.abs.gov.au/AUSSTATS/abs@.nsf/ProductsbyCatalogue/BC7AC812771E8FEFCA2578680014F525?OpenDocument.

Australian Children's Education and Care Quality Authority. (2013). *National quality standard.* Retrieved 14 October 2015 from http://www.acecqa.gov.au.

Australian Government Department of Education and Training. (2013). *Australian early development census 2012 summary report November 2013*. Canberra, Australia: Commonwealth of Australia.

Australian Government Department of Education and Training. (2015). *Universal access to early childhood education*. Canberra, Australia: Commonwealth of Australia.

Australian Health Ministers' Advisory Council. (2009). *National framework for universal child and family health services*. Canberra, Australia: Commonwealth of Australia.

Brennan, D. (1994). *The politics of Australian child care: From philanthropy to feminism*. Melbourne, Australia: Cambridge University Press.

Council of Australian Governments. (2009a). *National partnership on early childhood education*. Canberra, Australia: Australian Government.

Council of Australian Governments. (2009b). *Protecting children is everyone's business: National framework for protecting Australia's children 2009–2020*. Canberra, Australia: Council of Australian Governments.

Department of Education, Employment and Workplace Relations. (2009). *Belonging, being and becoming: The early years learning framework for Australia*. Canberra, Australia: Commonwealth Government of Australia.

Department of Education, Employment and Workplace Relations (DEEWR). (2011). *Early Childhood Policy Agenda*. Retrieved 9 September 2011 from www.deewr.gov.au/Earlychildhood/Policy_Agenda/Pages/home.aspx.

Eurofound. (2015). *Promoting uptake of parental and paternity leave among fathers in the European Unions*. Luxembourg: Publications office of the European Union.

European Union. (2014a). *Poland: On the road to suitable solutions in family policy*. European Union: Platform for Investing in children. Retrieved 17 October 2015 from http://europa.eu/epic/countries/poland/index_en.htm.

European Union. (2014b). *Sweden: Successful reconciliation of work and family life*. European Union: Platform for Investing in children. Retrieved 17 October 2015 from http://europa.eu/epic/countries/sweden/index_en.htm.

Försäkringskassan. (2014). Förälder. Retrieved 20 December 2014 from https://www.forsakringskassan.se/privatpers/foralder

Garvis, S., & Pendergast, D. (2013). Perceptions of rebates for nanny care: An analysis of an online discussion. *Australasian Journal of Early Childhood, 38*(3), 105–111.

Guendelman, S., English, P., & Chavez, G. (2009). Juggling work and breastfeeding: Effects of maternity leave and occupational characteristics. *Pediatrics, 123*, 38–46.

Institute for a Competitive Workforce. (2010). *Why business should support early childhood education*. Washington, DC: Institute for a Competitive Workforce, US Chamber of Commerce.

Ireland, L. (2006). *When babies have teachers: A study of how three community based children's services employ early childhood teachers in infant–toddler programs*. Paper presented at Australian Association for Research in Education (AARE) Conference, University of South Australia.

Kurinij, N., Shiono, P.H., Ezrine, S.F., et al. (1989). Does maternal employment affect breast-feeding? *American Journal of Public Health, 79*, 1247–1250.

Manning, M., Garvis, S., Fleming, C., and Wong, G. (in press). *Teacher Qualifications and their Impact on the Quality of the Early Childhood Learning Environment: A Systematic Review – Protocol*. The Campbell Collaboration. http://www.campbellcollaboration.org/lib/project/313/.

36 Policy perspectives in Australia

McMullen, M., & Alat, K. (2002). Education matters in the nurturing of the beliefs of preschool caregivers and teachers. *Early Childhood Research and Practice, 4*(2). http://ecrp.uiuc.edu/v4n2/mcmullen.html

Mirkovic, K.R., Perrine, C.G., Sanlon, K.S., & Grummer-Strawn, L.M. (2014). Maternity leave duration and full-time/part time work status are associated with US mothers' ability to meet breastfeeding intentions. *Journal of Human Lactation, 30*(4), 416–419.

Moss, P. (2013). *Access to early childhood education in Australia*. Canberra, Australia: Australian government Institute of Family Studies. *Journal of Human Lactation.*

Nolan, A., & Rouse, E. (2013). Where to from here? Career choices of pre-service teachers undertaking a dual early childhood/primary qualification. *Australian Journal of Teacher Education, 38*(1), 1–10. http://dx.doi.org/10.14221/ajte.2013v38n1.8

Norris, D. (2010). Raising the educational requirements for teachers in infant toddler classrooms: Implications for institutions of higher education. *Journal of Early Childhood Teacher Education, 31*, 146–158.

Nuttall, J. (1992). *Women, capitalism and feminism: Workers' experiences in private and non-profit child care centers.* (Master of Education), University of Canterbury, Christchurch.

OECD. (2006). *Starting strong II: Early childhood education and care.* Paris: OECD.

OECD. (2013). *Education at a glance 2013 highlights.* Paris: OECD.

Preiss, B. (2015). Extra teachers required for kindergartens could hike fees for parents. *The Age*, 2 October 2015.

Productivity Commission. (2009). *Paid parental leave: Support for parents with newborn children, report no. 47.* Canberra, Australia: Commonwealth of Australia.

Productivity Commission. (2014a). *Child care and early childhood learning: Productivity commission draft report.* Canberra, Australia: Commonwealth of Australia.

Productivity Commission. (2014b). *Childcare and early childhood learning: Overview. Report No. 73.* Canberra, Australia: Commonwealth of Australia.

Roberts, J., & Kingston, B. (Eds.) (2001). *Maybanke. A women's voice: The collected works of maybanke selfe~wolstenholme~Anderson 1845–1927.* Avalon Beach, NSW: Ruskin Rowe Press.

Rouse, E. (2008). *New directions for early childhood education: An analysis of the Rudd Government's policy directions for early childhood education in Australia.* Melbourne: Victoria University.

Rouse, L., Morrissey, A.M., & Rahimi, M. (2012). Problematic placement: Pathways pre-service teachers' perspectives on their infant/toddler placement. *Early Years, 32*(1), 87–98.

Sarkadi, A., Kristiansson, R., Oberklaid, F., & Bremberg, S. (2008). Fathers' involvement and children's developmental outcomes: A systematic review of longitudinal studies. *Acta Paediatr, 97*, 153–158.

Sims, M. (2013). The importance of early years education. In D. Pendergast & S. Garvis (Eds.), *Teaching early years: Curriculum, pedagogy and assessment* (pp. 30–32). Crows Nest, NSW: Allen and Unwin.

Sims, M., & Hutchins, T. (2011). *Program planning for infants and toddlers: In search of relationships.* Castle Hill, NSW: Pademelon Press.

Sims, M., & Waniganayake, M. (2015). The role of staff in quality improvement in early childhood. *Journal of Education and Training Services, 3*(5), 187–194.

Smerdon, X. *Australian Gender Pay Gap Widening* (2 March 2015) Pro Bono Australia <http://www.probonoaustralia.com.au/news/2015/03/australian-gender-pay-gap-widening>.

Sums ion, J. (2007). Sustaining the employment of early childhood teachers in long day care: A case for robust hope, critical imagination and critical action. *Asia-Pacific Journal of Teacher Education, 35*, 311–327.

UNICEF. (2014). *Global nutrition targets 2025: Breastfeeding policy brief.* World Health Organisation. Retrieved 17 October from http://www.who.int/nutrition/publications/globaltargets2025_policybrief_breastfeeding/en/.

United Nations. (1989). *Convention on the rights of the child.* Retrieved 14 October 2015 from http://www.ohchr.org/en/professionalinterest/pages/crc.aspx.

Walker, S., Wachs, T., Grantham-McGregor, S., Black, M., Nelson, C., Huffman, S., . . . Richter, L. (2011). Inequality in early childhood: Risk and protective factors for early child development. *The Lancet, 378*, 1325–1338.

Chapter 3

Education perspectives in Australia

This chapter provides an overview of early childhood education within the Australian context. Starting with information about how many children attend early childhood settings, the chapter then moves to show the current changes in understanding of the child, before providing a summary of the first Australian Early Years Learning Framework. Teacher education and content within teacher education is also discussed. In the final section, current issues within the early childhood education context are raised and a critical reflection provided of key considerations. The final section also compares early childhood education to current movements in Hong Kong, considered one of the most competitive systems in the world for education.

Children in early childhood settings

The number of children attending childcare within Australia is quite significant and it is around half the population of children aged birth to 12 years. As of June 2014, The Australian Bureau of Statistics reported that around 48 per cent of children aged birth to 12 years (around 1.8 million) attended some type of childcare (Australian Bureau of Statistics, 2015). The current figures suggest that around 1.3 million children attend informal childcare and 919,400 children attend formal care. Around one-fifth of children (22 per cent) were usually cared for by a grandparent, while 14 per cent attended long day care, 7.8 per cent attended before- and after-school care and 2.5 per cent attended family day care.

Patterns of attendance in early childhood settings also varied based on the age of the child. For example, 22 per cent of children aged under two years attended formal childcare, while 32 per cent attended informal childcare. The highest overall care attendance was among two and three year olds, where 71 per cent usually attended childcare (54 per cent attended formal care and 36 per cent attended informal childcare). For school-aged children (those aged five years and over), 14 per cent usually attended formal care, while 32 per cent attended informal care.

The Australian Bureau of Statistics (2015) has also reported on trends of parent types. Children who had one parent were more likely to attend any form of childcare (57 per cent) compared to couple families (46 per cent). Again grandparents were identified as the most common source for informal childcare (22 per cent in couples families and 23 per cent in one-parent families). What the current statistics do show is that while some children are attending formal childcare arrangements, other groups of children draw upon informal care arrangements.

Children as active agents

Over the past few decades, a growing body of literature has developed examining children's perspectives of their own lives, following the emergence of the 'new social studies of childhood' (James, Jenks, & Prout., 1998) and the children's rights discourse (The United Nations Convention on the Rights of the Child, 1989). Children are therefore viewed as social actors who are experts in their own lives and understanding of the world (Kellett & Ding, 2004; Mauthner, 1997). This new approach towards childhood has also meant a methodological shift towards the emergence of 'participatory' involvement within early childhood education.

These changes have also influenced the way children's learning is viewed. In particular, contemporary perspectives of children's learning are influenced by sociocultural theory, postmodernism, the sociology of childhood, poststructuralist theory and the reconceptualising early childhood movement. All of these contemporary perspectives recognise the "meaning-making competences of children as a basis for learning" (Malaguzzi, 1998, p. 81). The child is therefore positioned as strong with agency on their own learning within intricate and rapidly changing contexts (Clarke & Moss, 2001; Dahlberg, Moss, & Pence, 2007; Gutierrex et al., 2007).

Sociocultural theory "challenges us to examine our ideas and assumptions about traditional early childhood practices to analyse how relevant and useful these are for children from diverse families and cultures" (Arthur et al., 2012, p.14). This perspective recognizes the family context as the site where children learn 'cultural tools' (Vygotsky, 1978). It is for this reason that the social interactions of family life have become highly significant (Rogoff, 2003). For example, in the family context children will learn about having a meal, interacting with others, shopping and working. Children learn how to look, talk, act and think from participating in the family practices.

Under this perspective, learning differs for each child and needs to be understood within particular cultural and social contexts (Rogoff, 2003). Through engagement with families and communities, children establish their 'funds of knowledge' (Moll et al., 1992), becoming knowledgeable and skilled in ideas that are practised by their family. Sociocultural theorists suggest children therefore learn best when the curriculum is connected to their everyday lives.

Postmodernism perspectives identify changes in society while poststructural perspectives recognise transformation for each person (Mac Naughton, 2003).

40 Education perspectives in Australia

Both perspectives explain concepts of 'family' and 'community' as contexts for children's learning. Both focus on social practice through habitus, social capital and social field based on Bourdieu (1993) and/or 'discourse' based on Foucault (1978).

With a postmodern perspective, there is considered no single pathway of development for every child and there is no corresponding set of appropriate practices. Some therefore argue that learning should only be understood within local contexts (Grieshaber & Cannella, 2001; Mac Naughton, 2003). Postmodern theorists challenge taken-for-granted assumptions and the privileging of certain domains such as developmental psychology and work to "expand the range of perspectives possible for early childhood education" (Grieshaber & Cannella, 2001, p. 4).

Poststructuralist perspectives "address the complexities of the relationship between the child, the adult and their cultural context . . . [and] focus attention on the constitutive roles of gender, race, class and disability in children's learning and development" (Mac Naughton, 1995, p. 36). Poststructural theorists believe people have agency in their lives, so they are shaped not only by their environment but by their own identities and actions. Both postmodern and poststructural theorists argue that everyone has multiple identities that are socioculturally constructed, shifting and multifaceted (Dahlberg et al., 2007).

The similarity between the perspectives is that they support the view that images of children are created by communities and differ based on culture, context and period of time. Arthur et al. (2012, p. 20) suggest "the fact that children's lives differ in different cultures and in different centuries supports the view that images of children are created by communities". All of the perspectives recognise the rapid changes taking place in children's worlds and challenge dominant perspectives. In practice contemporary theories are employed in early childhood settings when educators find ways to work with children and families that (Arthur et al., 2012, p. 20):

- Engage in reflective practice, critical action and change
- Understand the importance of cultural contexts in children's learning
- Respect diversity and focus on equity and social justice
- Build effective partnerships with families, children and communities
- Enhance relationships and collaborative learning environments
- Focus on dispositions and processes of learning
- Provide meaningful curriculum that connects to children's social worlds and extends learning
- Engage in intentional teaching, drawing on a repertoire of pedagogies
- Document children's learning in ways that acknowledge children's strengths and make children's thinking visible to children and staff

Young children under these perspectives are considered competent and capable human beings. They also have many strengths and are able to communicate their understanding of the world through active meaning-making. Young children are able to participate in the world around them and interact with people and objects, allowing them to be seen and heard as active citizens.

Being, belonging and becoming: early years learning framework for Australia

Over the past decade, there has been an emergence around the world of Early Years Curriculum and Learning Frameworks, highlighting the complex nature early childhood plays within the political landscape. However, according to curriculum theorists, questions must always be asked of relationalities, discourses and silences (Sumison & Wong, 2011). Dillion (2009, p. 347) suggests the starting point for questions about curriculum should focus on "who, whom, what, where, when, why, how and what results". The chapter will return to these questions after providing information about the Australian context.

In 2010 the first Learning Framework for Australia was introduced, called *Being, belonging and becoming: Early Years Learning Framework for Australia* (DEEWR, 2009). While it was the first national document, states and territories had been providing early childhood curriculum frameworks for prior-to school settings. The aim of the national document was to extend the learning occurring in early childhood services for children from birth to five years across all of Australia. According to the Framework (DEEWR, p. 5) the aim is to:

> form the foundation for ensuring that children in all early childhood education and care settings experience quality teaching and learning. It has a specific emphasis on play-based learning and recognizes the importance of communication and language (including early literacy and numeracy) and social and emotional development. The Framework has been designed for use by early childhood educators working in partnership with families, children's first and most influential educators.

The document is based on the United Nations Convention on the Rights of the Child (United Nations, 1989), acknowledging that all children have a right to an education and that an education lays a foundation for the rest of a child's life to maximize their ability, and respects their family, cultural and other identities and languages. The Convention also recognizes a child's right to play and be active citizens in the world around them.

In broad terms, the Framework has also been linked with the *Melbourne Declaration on Education Goals for Young Australians* (MCEETYA, 2008) by supporting Goal 2 and acknowledging that all young Australians can become successful learners, confident and creative individuals and active and informed citizens.

The Framework characterizes children's lives by three terms: *belonging, being* and *becoming*. These are defined within the Framework as (DEEWR, 2009, p.7):

- Experiencing belonging – knowing where and with whom you belong – is integral to human existence. Children belong first to a family, a cultural group, a neighbourhood and a wider community. Belonging acknowledges children's interdependence with others and the basis of relationships in defining identities. In early childhood, and throughout life, relationships are crucial to a sense of belonging. Belonging is central to being and becoming in that it shapes who children are and who they can become.

- Being recognizes the significance of the here and now in children's lives. It is about the present and them knowing themselves, building and maintaining relationships with others, engaging with life's joys and complexities, and meeting challenges in everyday life. The early childhood years are not solely preparation for the future but also about the present.
- Children's identities, knowledge, understandings, capacities, skills and relationships change during childhood. They are shaped by many different events and circumstances. Becoming reflects this process of rapid and significant change that occurs in the early years as young children learn and grow. It emphasizes learning to participate fully and actively in society.

The Framework consists of five learning outcomes for children's learning from birth to five years. A learning outcome is considered a "skill, knowledge or disposition that educators can actively promote in early childhood settings, in collaboration with children and families" (DEEWR, 2009, p. 8). The five learning outcomes are:

1   Children have a strong sense of identity.
2   Children are connected with and contribute to their world.
3   Children have a strong sense of wellbeing.
4   Children are confident and involved learners.
5   Children are effective communicators.

The five outcomes provide broad directions for early childhood educators in their curriculum decision making and provide information for planning, implementing and evaluating quality within the early childhood setting.

The Framework also places children's learning at the core and consists of three related elements: principles, practice and learning outcomes.

The Framework is also unique in that it draws upon a number of different theories in regards to pedagogy, including sociocultural theories, socio-behaviourist theories, critical theories and poststructuralist theories. The Framework draws on a range of different perspectives and theories, allowing educators to reflect on their relationships with others and their ways of working.

There are five principles that reflect contemporary theories and research evidence on practice to assist children. These are (DEEWR, 2009, p. 13):

1   Secure, respectful and reciprocal relationships
2   Partnerships
3   High expectations and equity

4 Respect for diversity
5 Ongoing learning and reflective practice

The principles are underpinned by pedagogical practice to promote children's learning. The suggested practices are (DEEWR, 2009, p. 14):

- Adopting holistic approaches
- Being responsive to children
- Planning and implementing learning through play
- Intentional teaching
- Creating physical and social learning environments that have a positive impact on children's learning
- Valuing the cultural and social contexts of children and their families
- Providing for continuity in experiences and enabling children to have successful transition
- Assessing and monitoring children's learning to inform provision and to support children in achieving learning outcomes

The Framework was developed in four stages, beginning with a literature review of curriculum and learning frameworks for early childhood education (Wilks et al., 2008), followed by a commissioned paper to outline possible directions for the Framework (Edwards, Fleer, & Nuttal, 2008). The final two stages involved a draft and trial version of the Framework. In the final stages, a national consortium was awarded a competitive tender to the implementation. One of the members of the team suggests however (Sumison & Wong, 2011) that given the compressed timeline for the Framework development, trial and then the complex political negotiations associated with the Council of Australian Government's initiatives (Moon & Sharman, 2003) "that any easily reached points of agreement were eagerly seized upon, with little opportunity for subsequent in-depth, critical scrutiny" (Sumison & Wong, 2011, p. 29).

One particular aspect of the Framework that has also been discussed in the research literature in the reference to the spiritual dimension of children's lives, learning and diverse contexts (Grajczonek, 2012). According to the research of Grajczonek (2012, p. 152), this was:

> the first time at the Australian Federal Government level there was an official educational document that acknowledged the spiritual dimensions of children's lives and learning, advocating that holistic approaches to children's learning must include attending to the spiritual, as well as the physical and cognitive aspects. The document also assigns responsibilities to early childhood educators related to this spiritual dimension.

However Grajczonek (2012) also notes that while the document mentioned spirituality, there was no explicit detail about the actual nature of children's spirituality, the spiritual aspects of their learning and the nature of beliefs and values. She further highlights that such an omission is surprising, given Australia's increasing religiously diverse society. From this emerge differences in understanding 'belonging' and if this refers more to culture and not religion. Grajczonek (2012, p. 158) articulates that it is "important to understand and honour the other, not only in terms of cultural diversity but also in terms of religious diversity". She concludes with a need for educators to take a more holistic approach not only in terms of the child's learning, but also in the actual meaning of the terms belonging, being and becoming.

Another issue to emerge within the academic literature has been the concept of 'intentional teaching' within the Framework (Leggett & Ford, 2013). In the Framework, intentional teaching is defined as "educators being deliberate, purposeful and thoughtful in their decisions and actions. Intentional teaching is the opposite of teaching by rote or continuing with traditions simply because things have always been done that way" (DEEWR, 2009, p. 15). Leggett and Ford (2013, p. 43) argue that "what is lacking in the EYLF documents is a focus on a broader definition for intentionality that explores both the intended teaching acts of educators and the intentional learning of children". In their study they interviewed six early childhood educators and found that intentional teaching was routinely discussed only in the context of whole group sessions where knowledge acquisition was the primary aim. Leggett and Ford (2013) conclude with a call for a stronger recognition of the child as an intentional learner to help resolve current misunderstandings about intentionality.

Nevertheless, the Framework has been both celebrated and critiqued since implementation by policy makers, researchers and educators. A space has emerged within the research literature to interrogate and problematize the role of learning frameworks and their provision for quality programs for children. Such spaces can be seen as useful as they open up possibilities for further dialogue and encourage a "lively culture of professional inquiry and debate" (DEEWR, 2009, p. 13). It is through such dialogue that shared understandings can be developed.

My time, our place: framework for school-age care in Australia

In 2011, a Framework was also created for school-age care in Australia, part of the early childhood sector, entitled *My time, our place* Framework for School Age Care in Australia (DEEWR, 2011). The Framework has been designed for use by school-age care educators working in partnership with children, their families and the community, including schools. It represents Australia's first national framework for school-age care to be used by school-age care educators, and aims to extend and enrich children's wellbeing and development in school-age care settings.

This Framework is linked to the Early Years Learning Framework and extends the principles, practices and outcomes to the contexts and age range of the children and young people who attend school-age care settings. The Frameworks states that (DEEWR, 2011):

> In school age care settings educators collaborate with children to provide play and leisure opportunities that are meaningful to children and support their wellbeing, learning and development. School age care settings pay attention to the needs and interests of individual children within a context that promotes collaboration and active citizenship. Children in school age care settings have choice and control over their learning as they collaborate with educators to extend their life skills and develop dispositions towards citizenship.

The Framework acknowledges the importance of play and leisure in children's learning and development and that their learning is not limited to any particular time or place. Developing life skills and a sense of enjoyment are emphasized. The Framework recognizes the importance of social and emotional development and communication in learning through play and leisure, and it forms the foundation for ensuring that children in all school-age care settings engage in quality experiences for rich learning, personal development and citizenship opportunities (DEEWR, 2011).

Outside school hours care providers are also subject to the same quality checks by the Australian Children's Education and Care Quality Authority (ACECQA). They are required to document children's learning and provide meaningful learning experiences.

Becoming a teacher

In Australia, early childhood is overseen by ACECQA. Their role is to support the improvement of early childhood provision and quality. Part of their responsibility is the approval of programs for early childhood teachers. Universities submit an application and fee to ACECQA for approval of their teacher education program. Initially, all university programs were approved, but they had to be re-accredited with specific guidelines by 2017. This meant that, under new requirements, there had to be specific guidelines for birth to three years mapping and assignments. The application requires justification of alignment with guidelines for curriculum of what should be learnt. The curriculum content summary is listed in Table 3.1 (ACECQA, 2014, p. 5).

The above content does not specifically mention the education and care of infants and toddlers (or any age group) for bachelor degree and master's degree programs. However, the education and care of infants and toddlers is specifically mentioned by ACECQA for lower-ranked qualifications such as diploma and certificate qualifications.

There are also requirements to be met for practical experience (also known as practicum and professional experience) during teacher education programs (i.e. with children aged birth to five years of age). This experience occurs in licensed

46 Education perspectives in Australia

Table 3.1 Content within Early Childhood Teacher Education Programs

Psychology and child development,	*Teaching pedagogies,*
such as: • Learning, development and care • Language development • Social and emotional development • Child health, wellbeing and safety • Early intervention • Diversity, difference and inclusiv ity • Learners with special needs • Transitions and continuity of learning (including transition to school) **Education and curriculum studies,** such as: • Early Years Learning Framework • The Australian curriculum • Numeracy, science and technology • Language and literacy • English as an additional language • Social and environmental education • Creative arts and music • Physical and health education • Curriculum planning, programming and evaluation	such as: • Alternative pedagogies and curriculum approaches • Play-based pedagogies • Guiding behaviour/engaging young learners • Teaching methods and strategies • Children with diverse needs and backgrounds • Working with children who speak languages other than, or in addition to, English • Contemporary society and pedagogy **Family and community contexts,** such as: • Developing family and community perspectives • Multicultural education • Aboriginal and Torres Strait Islander perspectives • Socially inclusive practice • Culture, diversity and inclusion **History and philosophy of early childhood,** such as: • Historical and comparative perspectives • Contemporary theories and practice • Ethics and professional practice. **Early childhood professional practice,** such as: • Leadership • Management and administration • Professional identity and development • Advocacy • Research

Source: ACECQA, 2014

centers or schools under the supervision of a qualified teacher (for example in Queensland, Tasmania and Western Australia this can occur in school). For master degree programs, pre-service teachers are required to complete 60 days. The master degree has time requirements based on age range. For example, placements must include a minimum of 10 days of practical experience with children aged birth to two years. Placements must also occur with children aged three to five years and above five years. Exact number of days across age ranges depends on if the program is for birth to five years, birth to eight years or birth to 12 years. This suggests variation in placement contexts.

Early childhood teachers can be qualified in two ways: (1) a four-year undergraduate bachelor degree; (2) or, an 18-month to two-year postgraduate master degree – providing the student has a non-education bachelor degree. Recent Australian government data (COAG, 2009) has highlighted a shortage of qualified early childhood teachers, and thus, the government has a mandate for more teachers, in this sector, to be trained in tertiary institutions.

The Australian government mandate on employing degree qualified early childhood teachers has come from overseas research showing links between educational qualification and the quality of early childhood education programs (Sylvaat al., 2011). Qualified early childhood staff are particularly important in the early years, especially for infants and toddlers (Duncan & Magnuson, 2013; Ireland, 2006). Thus, there is an assumption underpinning the Australian National Quality Framework that qualified early childhood teachers will make a difference to the quality in services provided, thus translating into better outcomes for children (Nolan & Rouse, 2013). Further, research supports that a qualified workforce will improve children's outcomes across all age ranges (especially infants and toddlers), as better education in the early years provides the necessary skills for children to successfully negotiate key transitions in their lives (Manning, 2014).

Australian government requirements also demand that qualified teachers work with older-aged children as part of a universal access agreement that allows all children, in the year before schooling, access to an early childhood teacher (Rouse, Morrissey, & Rahimi, 2012). Previous Australian research suggests that qualified teachers in childcare centers end up working with older children; while diploma- and certificate-qualified educators (or sometimes unqualified staff) work with the younger children (Rouseet al., 2012). Therefore, younger children tend to receive little time with a qualified early childhood teacher. Recent evidence (Nolan & Rouse, 2013) suggests that this may be due, in part, to pre-service early childhood teachers' preference to work with older children as opposed to younger children as well as the pay and working conditions in long day care.

In a recent Australian survey of early childhood pre-service teachers in one Australian institution, Rouse et al. (2012) noted many comments from students dissatisfied about the infant/toddler practicum in which they had engaged. Participants commented that they 'already knew' how to work with this age group, and that they aspired to work with older children. Rouse et al. (2012, p. 97) concluded that " . . . as it currently stands, the infant/toddler practicum, while essential in building competent early childhood teachers, is problematic and a challenge". Responses indicated dissatisfaction with the quality of supervision, the absence of teacher-mentors, and the lack of opportunities to practice new approaches. However, Australian research also reports infant and toddler placement being a positive experience for students. Thorpe et al. (2011) explored the beliefs of pre-service teachers in their third year of study of a Bachelor of Education (early childhood specialisation).

In another Australian study, a content analysis of bachelor-degree early childhood teacher education programs (aged birth to eight years) highlighted that infants and toddlers received limited attention compared to older children (Garvis et al., 2013). While the range of early childhood teacher education programs claim to have a broad reach (from birth to eight years of age), typically there is a light touch in the earlier years (0–3 years) (Garvis et al., 2013). Garvis and Manning (2015) made a similar finding within master-level programs in a study of content to become a qualified early childhood teacher. Garvis and Lemon (2015) together with Ireland (2006) note that there is not a strong tradition of teachers being involved in infant/toddler programs across Australia. Similar findings have been reported in the United States with birth to three years also receiving little recognition and attention over the past 10 years (Recchia & Shin, 2010). There is also a perception in the United States, and some Westernised countries, that the educational preparation required of infant and toddler 'caregivers' is less rigorous than that required of 'teachers' of older children (Recchia & Shin, 2010).

Nordic countries also appear to have problems with infant and toddler teacher education programs with teachers in Iceland, Sweden and Norway highlighting a number of dilemmas when working with very young children – suggesting that the youngest of children in care were marginalised (Alverstad et al., 2014). Early childhood teachers appear to have a limited understanding of what professional work with young children included, with attitudes of "just changing nappies" sometimes expressed (Alvestad et al., 2014, p. 682).

The focus on older children (three years onwards) may be because of traditional views about infants (birth to 12 months) who are perceived as incapable and dependent (Cannella, 1997), often leading caregiving adults to underestimate their potential as learners. This focus, however, has hopefully changed or is in a state of transition given the recent focus within the Early Years Learning Framework (DEEWR, 2009), which highlights children as capable and competent in meaning-making. In early childhood teacher education, it is important that such views about children are challenged. Garvis et al. (2013) suggests that in order to overcome this deficit view, what is required is teacher transformation in the Australian early childhood education sector. Agbenyega (2012, 142) notes that as "pre-service early childhood teachers do not know what to expect in child care and kindergartens; a transformational approach to teacher preparation is crucial for preparing them to adapt to changing pedagogical and contextual situations". By allowing pre-service teachers to experience the learning of infants and toddlers, they are able to connect their learning and understanding of young children across all early childhood settings, linking understanding of how children transition between prior to formal (i.e., childcare and kindergarten) and formal schooling (i.e., primary school). Garvis and Manning (2015, p. 173) also recommended a number of future considerations for early childhood teacher education including:

- Carefully focussing on the required period of time for pre-service teachers to gain the knowledge and practical experience required to work with infants and toddlers (currently a minimum of 10 days) and ensuring that this time is comparable to what is currently required for older children. Questions need to be asked if 10 days of professional experience is enough, or more is needed to ensure students develop the necessary knowledge and skills.

- Ensuring universities across Australia collaborate in an effort to develop content that is consistently taught to future educators of infants and toddlers. This will provide consistency in learning about infants and toddlers and reduce the current identified problems of portability of qualifications across Australia.
- More studies into effective early childhood teacher education programs for infants and toddlers within Australia are required to enhance quality. Given the variation in the delivery of programs, a better understanding is needed of graduate capability and competence. This may include initial assessment of student knowledge and understanding upon graduation.
- More studies are also needed exploring the views of teacher educators, pre-service teachers and recent graduates about their experiences within university programs, specifically with a focus on infants and toddlers. It would be interesting to also see if pre-service teachers had increased efficacy for working with infants and toddlers if they spent more than 10 days in a childcare setting.
- Given that this program showed programs in a state of transition, graduates from these programs may have less of an understanding of infants and toddlers compared to students in programs that have been re-accredited. If this is true, professional learning is required for recent graduates regarding infants and toddlers.

Other tensions in early childhood education

Within Australian early childhood education, other tensions also emerge around actual learning and skills learnt within early childhood settings and the perspectives and skills of the current Australian early childhood workforce. A snapshot of these issues are provided, but all require further dialogue within Australian early childhood education by educators, managers and policy makers.

Schoolification and transition to school

Within Australia, there has been also focus within the transition of children from early childhood services to the first year of schooling. This has meant how children and their families can be supported as they move from one educational institution to another educational institution. On the New South Wales Public Schools (2011) website, a transition to school program is defined as a set of planned activities or a process established collaboratively by a range of players that make starting school as successful as possible for children, families and teachers.

One concern within early childhood education has been the focus on school readiness, leading sometimes to the 'schoolification' within early childhood settings. The philosophy of school readiness is related to schools' practices and policies in assisting children and families to transition from preschool to primary school (Dockett & Perry, 2008). In one Australian study, Noel (2011) explored transition programs to identify key aspects within each program. Noel (2011) identified communication between preschool teachers and school administrators or teachers as an area of major concern. This resulted in a lack of optimal communication among educators. Noel (2011, p. 50) commented that "without such contact, there is strong potential for misunderstandings between preschool teachers and primary school teachers on topics such as expectations for school readiness and the requirements of a play-based curriculum".

The push down of the Australian National Curriculum (beginning from five years of age) is also starting to appear to influence early childhood education. Early formalised literacy and numeracy development appear to have started to gain ground within Australian early childhood education. What this means is structured formalised learning (rather than through a play-based approach) for literacy and numeracy to develop the skills needed for children before they start school. Especially within the first years of school (children aged five years), it may be difficult to find elements of play-based learning.

Educators' perspectives of diversity and difference upon their pedagogy

Research has found that immigrant children experience an informal socialisation process into Australian culture and the use of English within Australian early childhood settings (Amigo, 2012), however the children are not encouraged to keep their cultural and linguistic background (Buchori & Dobinson, 2015). This may be because of different understandings about culture, ethnicity, equity and participation (McInerney, 2003). Moreover, studies have also highlighted a need for improving educator's abilities to understand, respect and respond to diverse situations in the early childhood classroom (Souto-Manning & Mitchell, 2009). In a recent Australian study, Buchori and Dobinson (2015) highlighted troubling findings from a study of early childhood teachers. Firstly, they found that while early childhood teachers were positive towards multiculturalism, they also saw it as a burden for children's learning. They found that the children's experiences and cultural knowledge were not always recognised as a resource. The importance of conformity was also exhibited by the early childhood teachers. The dominant culture was used as a tool by which to measure the "values of other peoples' culture" (Buchori & Dobinson, 2015, p. 77). The early childhood teachers would therefore take on a parent role for the immigrant children. This also led to a 'fear of failure' from the teachers, that represented not only the students failing, but also their own failings to line managers and the students' parents. "Despite the best intentions of the teachers, cultural diversity was celebrated in a perfunctory manner (Buchori & Dobinson, 2015, p. 77). It was recommended that increased

Education perspectives in Australia 51

meta-cultural sensitivity and awareness on the part of early childhood teachers was needed to enhance confidence and provide opportunities for dialogue between families and educators.

Educational change

To help understand the change occurring within the education system in early childhood since 2010, researchers have adapted an educational change model for early childhood education (Garvis et al., 2013) that was originally developed for the middle years of schooling. The model has been helpful for the early childhood sector, especially in the state of Victoria where it was developed, in understanding early years reform. One of the guiding features has also been the importance of developing 'lifelong learning' for both children and early childhood professionals.

One of the distinct features of the change model are the three phases of change: initiation, development and consolidation. The three phases require significant time for core component changes and can takes between eight to 17 years (longer than most expected reform changes within reform schedules). The three phases are able to describe indicative levels of engagement and suggest strategies for ongoing professional learning. The model also has value for an individual, for an early childhood setting and at the systematic level. According to Garvis et al. (2013, p. 87):

> At an individual level it can be used to assist a person to determine the stage of reform at which they are operating by reflecting on their understanding and practices. Similarly, in a specific site the phase of reform can be determined by auditing the evidence presented across the site. At a systematic level the guidance required to scaffold individuals and sites to achieve reform can be tailored by utilising the comments of the phases as an audit tool.

The Educational Change Model is represented in Figure 3.1 below.

During the Initiation phase reforming organizations are characterised by activities that include goal setting (for example, development of vision statements) and developing buy-in and information dissemination of the new reforms, what they entail and how they'll be achieved (Pendergast, 2006). The focus for individuals is on understanding the new reforms and the implications for changes to their thinking, language and practices. The Initiation phase typically extends from one to two years.

During the Development phase, typically from years two to five, individuals and groups are deepening their understanding of the reforms and implementing more and more new practices in accordance with the new reforms. This stage of exploration and experimentation yields many successes, but inevitably leads to some failed trials and experiments. This can sometimes result in frustration, despair and despondency with the new reforms and is accompanied by decreases

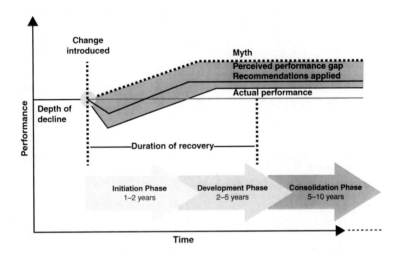

Figure 3.1 Educational Change Model for Early Childhood Education (Garvis et al., 2013, p. 87)

in performance and perceived efficacy. This is identified in the literature as an implementation dip (Pendergast & Main, 2011).

During the Consolidation phase, typically from years five to 10, individual and group understanding of the reform is much more closely aligned and practices have been largely bedded down. Organisations are further deepening their knowledge, and the language and practices are becoming more automatic and widespread within the organisation. Individual reliance on experts and leadership decreases as their own expertise increases. Reform efforts have largely disappeared by this phase with the expectation that individuals are able to continuously improve independent of external assistance as individuals move towards a more expert knowledge and practice base.

As participants move throughout the phases of reform, their understanding of the reform and the ability to implement reform changes significantly over time. Since each phase is different, the professional learning needs of the participants changes, suggesting learning packages needed to be tailor-made to the current needs of the participant.

One of the myths with educational reform is that the introduction of a new policy or procedure will result in immediate improvement in performance. In Figure 3.1 you can see the dotted line that represents the myth of perceived change. In reality, the actual performance dips as participants re-establish who they are and what their current work is. "Applying appropriate recommendations can reduce the depth of the decline and also reduce the duration of recovery"

(Garvis et al., 2013, p.88). Support is needed to assist participants through each of the phases. As Pendergast et al. (2005, p. 85) note:

> Even with dynamic and consistent leadership ... the effort required to maintain the momentum of reform is enormous, and it is not uncommon for enthusiasm to wane, especially if funding is not sufficient to meet adequately all of the very high costs usually associated with the quality of renewal required. Most ... in the Development phase undergo a significant 'dip' in their implementation efforts and the efficiency with which they are able to operate.

This 'typical pattern' can be represented diagrammatically as in Figure 3.2. The 'fast-tracked pattern' is represented in Figure 3.3.

The early childhood profession is able to fast-track reform processes if it has access to optimal conditions. This can occur when several key factors are aligned and sustained (Garvis et al., 2013 p. 89):

- Team membership across several years
- Congenial, philosophically aligned dynamics among team members
- Sensitive and sustained leadership
- Early adoption and shared risk-taking among members who challenge each other to extend themselves
- A strong emphasis on team problem-posing and problem solving
- Effective use of research in evidence-based planning

What this means is that given the government's introduction of reform from 2010 onwards, actual reform is still within the development phase within Australian early childhood education. The next phase will be consolidation that will take up to another five years for reform to be acted upon and implemented efficiently throughout the early childhood sector. Such progression is also dependent on the

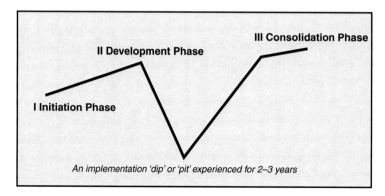

Figure 3.2 Typical Pattern of Educational Change (Garvis et al., 2013, p. 87)

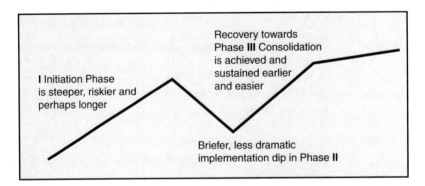

Figure 3.3 Fast-Tracked Pattern of Educational Change (Garvis et al., 2013, p. 88)

key factors listed above, especially around leadership and working as teams within early childhood settings. It is only through team membership within early childhood settings that all participants can move forward, increasing levels of understanding, skills as well as confident and personal identity as an early childhood professional.

Comparisons with other countries

Hong Kong

In 2013 to 2014, there were a total of 969 kindergartens and childcare centers in Hong Kong (Education Bureau, 2014). Most kindergartens offer half-day classes (three hours) while childcare centers offer whole-day programs.

Hong Kong has been identified as one of the most competitive education systems in the world in which examinations are heavily used (Education Commission, 2000; Watkins, 2009). Elitism is therefore socially and culturally encouraged, where education is considered a means for upward social mobility (Wong & Rao, 2015). Ng (2009) states that 34 per cent of students in primary and secondary schools in Hong Kong attend cram schools, while around 50 per cent of primary school students have tutors. Tutorial classes for learning to read and early mathematics are also common for kindergarten children, starting when children are six months of age. Given such a focus on education, nearly all children aged three to six years attend preschool programs, even though early childhood education is not compulsory in Hong Kong (Audit Commission, 2013). According to Rao et al. (2009), Hong Kong parents also perceive early childhood education programs as preparatory courses for primary schools.

A report was published by the Committee on Free Kindergarten Education (2015) entitled *Children First, Right Start for All*. The report provided recommendations about the proposed access to provide free kindergarten services for all children in Hong Kong, allowing 15 years of free education. The report suggested that funding should occur for the half-day programs. They also recommend that kindergarten teachers should be required to have a degree level to further enhance quality. Other suggestions included decreasing current teacher to children ratios from one teacher to 15 children, to one teacher to 12 children. Another suggestion has been the creation of a *Teacher Competencies Framework* and a *Principal Competencies Framework*. The report is still being considered by the government, however it does show the focus on quality improvement as well as providing universal access to children aged 3–6 years, while still not making early childhood education compulsory.

Within Hong Kong, there has been the same pre-primary curriculum since 2007, entitled *Guide to the Pre-Primary Curriculum*. According to the Education Bureau (2015), the curriculum emphasises that early childhood education lays the foundation for lifelong learning and whole person development. A focus should be made on both children's development and children's learning. Within the curriculum there are four objectives:

- Physical development
- Cognitive and language development
- Affective and social development
- Aesthetic development

The objectives are achieved through six learning areas, which consist of:

- Physical fitness and health
- Language
- Early mathematics
- Science and technology
- Self and society
- Arts

The intention of the curriculum is to provide opportunities to nurture the whole child, providing a well-rounded development program to prepare children for life as well as lay foundations for future learning.

To ensure that pre-primary settings are improving quality, performance indicators for pre-primary institutions have also been introduced. The performance indicators are grouped into two categories: process indicators and outcomes indicators. Process indicators consist of management and organisation, learning and teaching and the support given to children and the school culture. Outcomes indicators consist of children's development. The intention is to promote and further enhance the quality of kindergartens in Hong Kong.

From the Hong Kong system it is clear that there are similarities and differences to the Australian context:

- Universal access is provided in both countries, however early childhood education is not compulsory. The time allocation appears similar (around

15 hours a week). Only primary school and secondary school are compulsory in both countries.

- Both countries are focused on quality improvement within early childhood education, focusing on the quality of early childhood services, as well as children's outcomes. Both countries have systems to review quality based on standards or performance indicators.
- Both countries are committed to improving staff qualifications for teachers working with children three years and up. A degree-qualified teacher is preferred in both contexts.
- The curriculum and focus of the curriculum is different in the countries. The Hong Kong curriculum is prescribed with set developmental areas and learning areas. The Australian Framework incorporates a number of different philosophies and approaches, working towards learning outcomes. The Hong Kong curriculum has also a long establishment in the early childhood system, while the Australian Learning Framework is the first for the nation.
- Children's attendance rates in early childhood settings for Hong Kong are significantly higher than Australia. This could be due to the different function and perception of early childhood education. Early learning (from six months of age) appears a strong focus with Hong Kong parents.
- Both countries are yet to consider the youngest of children, aged birth to three years, within early childhood policy. While universal access is provided for children three years and up, no government commitment has been provided for the youngest of children with universal access.

Key reflections on the education perspective

Over the last decades there has been a growth in early childhood education and care, largely representing the changing philosophies of children and a shared understanding within education of children's rights. This has led to changes in practice and policies with young children.

In Australia there have been many important steps to help enhance the quality of early childhood education and care. Children have been considered active agents, recognising children as competent and capable. This has included the introduction of the first *Australian Early Years Learning Framework*, requirements for qualified teachers and a general respect shown for children as confident and capable. The education perspective also acknowledges that change may not be instantaneous and requires years of implementation to be successful. Educators, leaders and policy makers need to be aware that implementing change is not simple, and requires strong support for professional learning.

While there have been many changes taking place within the education landscape, there have also been emerging criticisms. These have surrounded the *Australian Early Years Learning Framework*, content within early childhood teacher education focusing on the youngest of children and concern shown around the schoolification of early childhood education, enhancing understanding about diversity and difference and spirituality within education. It is important for educators, researchers and policy makers to listen to concerns in order to develop better understandings of possible gaps and areas of need within education. By listening and engaging in dialogue, better ways of working and supporting children's learning and development can occur.

This chapter has also provided a snapshot of Hong Kong as a comparison to Australian early childhood education. While the two contexts share many similarities within their early childhood system, they also have many differences, including the participation rates of children as well as significant differences in the curriculum documents. Both countries however share a common interest on quality assessment and universal access. A comparison five years from now would be highly interesting, especially considering both countries have implemented recent changes within society for early childhood education and care.

Lastly, the number of children in formal and informal care contexts within Australia requires consideration, especially the number of children who may be cared for by another family member, such as a grandparent. The ABS (2015) suggested that around one in five children are cared for by a grandparent within early childhood education and care. If this statistic is true, it would be interesting to compare the learning experiences of children in early childhood centers compared to learning experiences with grandparents. Is one more beneficial than the other? How can grandparents be supported with the education and care of their grandchildren? Could more of a shared space be created between grandparents and formal early childhood services? As early childhood education becomes more prevalent within Australian society, such changes will be interesting to observe. The future appears promising, provided educational change is supported.

References

Agbenyega, J. (2012). How we view our theoretical competency: Early childhood pre-service teachers' self-evaluation of a professional placement experience. *Australasian Journal of Early Childhood, 37*(2), 141–147.

Alvestad, T., Bergem, H., Eide, B., Johansson, J.E., Os, E., Palmadottir, H., Pramling Samuelsson, I., & Winger, S. (2014). Challenges and dilemmas expressed by teachers working in toddler groups in the Nordic countries. *Early Childhood Development and Care, 184*(5), 671–688.

Amigo, M.F. (2012). Liminal but competent: Latin American migrant children and school in Australia. *Child Studies in Diverse Contexts, 2*(1), 61–75.

Arthur, L., Beecher, B., Death, E., Dockett, S., & Farmer, S. (2012). *Programming and planning in early childhood settings.* Sydney: Cengage Learning.

Audit Commission. (2013). *Pre-primary education voucher scheme (director of audit report no. 60).* Hong Kong: Hong Kong Audit Commission.

Australian Bureau of Statistics. (2015). *4202.0- Childhood education and care, Australia, June 2014.* Retrieved 22 October from http://www.abs.gov.au/ausstats/abs@.nsf/mf/4402.0.

58 Education perspectives in Australia

Australian Children's Education and Care Quality Authority. (ACECQA). (2014). *Qualification assessment information for organisation applicants*. Retrieved 5 January 2015 from http://www.acecqa.gov.au/Approval-of-early-childhood-education-programs.

Bourdieu, P. (1993). *Sociology in question*. London: Sage.

Buchori, S., & Dobinson, T. (2015). Diversity in teaching and learning: Practiitoners' perspectives in a multiultural early chidlhood setting in Australia. *Australasian Journal of Early Childhood, 40*(1), 71–79.

Cannella, G.S. (1997). *Deconstructing early childhood education: Social justice and revolution*. New York: Peter lang.

Clark, A., & Moss, P. (2001). *Listening to young children: The Mosaic approach*. London: National Children's Bureau.

Committee on Free Kindergarten Education. (2015). *Children first right start for all*. Retrieved 25 October 2015 from http://www.edb.gov.hk/en/edu-system/preprimary-kindergarten/kg-report/index.html.

Council of Australian Governments. (2009). *National partnership on early childhood education*. Canberra: Australian Government.

Dahlberg, G., Moss, P., & Pence, A. (2007). *Beyond quality in early childhood education and care: Postmodern perspectives*. London: Falmer Press.

Department of Education, Employment and Workplace Relations. (2009). *Belonging, being and becoming: The early years learning framework for Australia*. Canberra, Australia: Commonwealth Government of Australia.

Department of Education, Employment and Workplace Relations. (2011). *My time, our place: Framework for school age care in Australia*. Canberra, Australia: Commonwealth Government of Australia.

Dillon, J.T. (2009). The questions of curriculum. *Journal of Curriculum Studies, 41*(3), 343–359.

Dockett, S., & Perry, B. (2008). Starting school: A community endeavour. *Childhood Education, 85*(5), 274–281.

Duncan, G.J., & Magnuson, K. (2013). Investing in preschool programs. *The Journal of Economic Perspectives, 27*(2), 109–132.

Education Bureau. (2015). *Overview of kindergarten education in Hong Kong*. Retrieved 25 October 2015 from http://www.edb.gov.hk/en/edu-system/preprimary-kindergarten/overview/index.html.

Education Commission. (2000). *Learning for life, learning through life: Reform proposals for the education system in Hong Kong*. Hong Kong: Government Printer.

Edwards, S., Fleer, M., & Nuttall, J. (2008). *A research paper to inform the development of an early years learning framework for Australia*. Melbourne: Office for Children and Early Childhood Development, Department of Education and Early Childhood Development.

Foucault, M. (1978). *History of sexuality: An introduction*. London: Penguin.

Garvis, S., & Lemon, N. (2015). Enhancing the Australian early childhood teacher education curriculum about very young children. *Early Child Development and Care, 185*(4), 547–561.

Garvis, S., Lemon, N., Pendergast, D., & Yim, B. (2013). A content analysis of early childhood teachers' theoretical and practical experiences with infants and toddlers in Australian teacher education programs. *Australian Journal of Teacher Education, 38*(9), 25–36.

Garvis, S., & Manning, M. (2015). Do master early childhood teacher education programs provide adequate coverage of infants and toddlers? A review of content. *Australian Journal of Teacher Education, 40*(8) 164–175.

Garvis, S., Pendergast, D., Twigg, D., Fluckiger, B., Kanasa, H., Phillips, C., Bishop, M., & Lockett, K. (2013). The victorian early years learning and development framework: Managing change in a complex environment. *Australasian Journal of Early Childhood, 38*(2), 86–94.

Grajcsonek, J. (2012). Interrogating the spiritual as constructed in belonging, being and becoming: The early years learning framework for Australia. *Australasian Journal of Early Childhood, 37*(1), 152–160.

Grieshaber, S., & Cannella, G. (2001). From identity to identities: Increasing possibilities in early childhood education. In S. Grieshaber & G. Cannella (Eds.), *Embracing identities in early childhood education: Diversity and possibilities.* (pp. 3–22). New York: Teachers College Press.

Gutierrez, K.D., Larson, J., Enciso, P., & Ryan, C. (2007). Discussing expanded spaces for learning. *Languages Arts, 85*(1), 69–77.

Ireland, L. (2006). *When babies have teachers: A study of how three community based children's services employ early childhood teachers in infant–toddler programs.* Paper presented at the Australian association for research in Education (AARE) Conference, University of South Australia.

James, A., Jenks, C., & Prout, A. (1998). *Theorising childhood.* Cambridge: Polity.

Kellett, M., & Ding, S. (2004). Middle childhood. In S. Fraser, V. Lewis, S. Ding, M. Kellet, & C. Robinsons (Eds.), *Doing research with children and young people* (pp. 161–174). London: The Open University.

Leggett, N., & Ford, N. (2013). A fine balance: Understanding the roles educators and children play as intentional teachers and intentional learners within the early years learning framework. *Australasian Journal of Early Childhood, 38*(4), 42–50.

MacNaughton, G. (1995). A post-structuralist analysis of learning in early childhood settings. In M. Fleer (Ed.), *DAPcentrism: Challenging developmentally appropriate practice.* Canberra: Australian Early Childhood Association.

Mac Naughton, G. (2003). *Shaping early childhood: Learners, curriculums and contexts.* Maidenhead: Open University Press.

Malaguzzi, L. (1998). History, ideas and basic philosophy. In C. Edwards, L. Gandini, & G. Foreman (Eds.), *The hundred languages of children* (pp. 49–97). Norwood: Ablex.

Manning, M. (2014). Developmental interventions on children and familial wellbeing. In S. Garvis & D. Pendergast (Eds.), *Health and well-being in the early years* (31–47). Cambridge: Cambridge University Press.

Mauthner, M. (1997). Methodological aspects of collecting data from children: Lessons from three research projects. *Children and Society, 11,* 16–28.

MCEETYA. (2008). *Melbourne declaration on educational goals for young Australians.* Retrieved 28 April 2009 from http://www.mceetya.edu.au/verve/_resources/National_Declaration_on_the_Educational_Goals_for_Young_Australians.pdf.

Mclnerney, V. (2003). *Multiculturalism in today's schools: Have teachers' attitudes changed over two decades?* Retrieved 15 June 2011 from www.aare.edu.au.

Moll, L., Amanti, C., Neff, D., & Gonzalez, N. (1992). Funds of knowledge for teaching: Using a qualitative approach to connect homes and classrooms. *Theory into Practice, 31*(2), 132–141.

Moon, J., & Sharman, C. (2003). *Australian politics and government: The commonwealth, the states and the territories.* Cambridge, UK, Cambridge University Press.

New South Wales Public Schools. (2011). *What is transition to school?* Retrieved 22 March 2013 from www.schools.new.edu.au.

Ng, Y-H. (2009). In Hong Kong, cram school teachers' image rivals pop stars. *The New York Times.*

Noel, Andrea (2011). Easing the transition to school: Administrators' descriptions of transition to school activities. *Australasian Journal of Early Childhood, 36*(4), 44–52.

Nolan, A., & Rouse, E. (2013). Where to from here? Career choices of pre-service teachers undertaking a dual early childhood/primary qualification. *Australian Journal of Teacher Education, 38*(1), 1–10.

Pendergast, D. (2006). Fast-tracking middle schooling reform: A model for sustainability. *Australian Journal of Middle Schooling, 6*(2), 13–18.

Pendergast, D., Flanagan, R., Land, R., Bahr, M., Mitchell, J., Weir, K., Noblett, G., Cain, M., Misich, T., Carrington, V., & Smith, J. (2005). *Developing lifelong learners in the middle years of schooling: A report about the practices, process, strategies and structures that best promote 'lifelong learning' and the development of 'lifelong learners' in the middle years of schooling.* Brisbane, Queensland: The University of Queensland.

Pendergast, D., & Main, K. (2011). Middle school reform: Constructing an audit tool for practical purposes. *Australian Journal of Middle Schooling, 11*(2), 4–10.

Rao, N., Ng, S.S.N., & Pearson, E.C. (2009). Preschool pedagogy: A fusion of traditional Chinese beliefs and contemporary notions of appropriate practice. In C.K.K. Chan & N. Rao (Eds.), *Revisiting the Chinese learner: Changing contexts, changing education* (pp. 255–279). Hong Kong: Comparative Education Research Centre, The University of Hong Kong.

Recchia, S.L., & Shin, M. (2010). 'Baby teachers': How pre-service early childhood students transform their conceptions of teaching and learning through an infant practicum. *Early Years: An International Journal of Research and Development, 30*(2), 135–145.

Rogoff, B. (2003). *The cultural nature of human development.* Oxford: Oxford University Press.

Rouse, L., Morrissey, A.M., & Rahimi, M. (2012). Problematic placement: Pathways pre-service teachers' perspectives on their infant/toddler placement. *Early Years, 32*(1), 87–98.

Souto-Manning, M., & Mitchell, C.H. (2009). The role of action research in fostering culturally responsive practices in a pre-school classroom. *Early Childhood Education Journal, 37*(4), 269–277.

Sumison, J., & Wong, S. (2011). Interrogating 'belonging' in belonging, being and becoming: The early years learning framework for Australia. *Contemporary Issues in Early Childhood, 12*(1), 28–45.

Sylva, K., Melhuish, E., Sammons, P., Siraj-Blatchford, I., & Taggart, B. (2011). *Early childhood matters: Evidence from the effective preschool and primary school education project.* London: Routledge.

Thorpe, K., Boyd, W.A., Ailwood, J., & Brownlee, J. (2011). Who wants to work in childcare? Pre-service early childhood teacher's consideration of work in the childcare sector. *Australasian Journal of Early Childhood, 36*(1), 85–94.

United Nations. (1989). *Convention on the rights of the child*. Retrieved 14 October 2015 from http://www.ohchr.org/en/professionalinterest/pages/crc.aspx.

Vygotsky, L. (1978). *Mind in society: The development of higher psychological processes.* Cambridge, MA: Harvard University Press.

Watkins, D.A. (2009). Motivation and competition in Hong Kong secondary schools: The students' perspective. In C.K.K. Chan & N. Rao (Eds.), *Revisiting the Chinese learner: Changing contexts, changing education* (pp. 71–88). Hong Kong: Comparative Education Research Centre, The University of Hong Kong.

Wilks, A., Nyland, B., Chancellor, B., & Elliot, S. (2008) *An Analysis of Curriculum/ Learning Frameworks for the Early Years (Birth to Age 8)*. East Melbourne: State of Victoria Department of Education and Early Child Development and Victorian Curriculum and Assessment Authority; http://www.deewr.gov.au/EarlyChildhood/ OfficeOfEarlyChildhood/sqs/Documents/AnalysisofCurriculum_Learning FrameworksfortheEarly.pdf.

Wong, J.S.M., & Rao, N. (2015). The evolution of early childhood education policy in Hong Kong. *International Journal of Child Care and Education Policy, 9*(3), 1–16.

Chapter 4

Economics perspectives in Australia

Recent international research suggests that high-quality early education is a long-term social and economic investment. Those involved in developing and implementing education policy have generally thought that such investment is limited to enhancing school readiness or acting as a way of closing the achievement gap. Economists, however, offer a further benefit. They propose that investments in early education may be considered an economic development strategy, concluding that such an investment yields a return that far exceeds the return on most public projects that are considered economic development. Economic analyses have attempted to show how investing in young children fosters individual productivity. This is particularly the case for children who live in poverty or are marginalised as a result of other developmental, social and environmental factors. Moreover, economists have attempted to establish a link between the development of cognitive and non-cognitive abilities and a productive workforce, arguing that the association between early experiences and later outcomes cannot be ignored. In short, economists propose that skills are accumulated. Family environments and the association between school and the family are also considered by economists to be an important determinant of educational success and skill formation. In sum, starting early and investing in institutions of education and care at critical transition points is an investment in the future economic development of a nation.

This chapter introduces early years educators, academics, students and practitioners to the insights offered by economists in the area of early childhood education and skills development nationally and internationally. The chapter summarises the theory underpinning the economic rationale for high-quality well-delivered early education, providing some evidence regarding potential economic returns. The chapter then goes on to unpack the argument regarding how investments in quality early childhood education can improve health outcomes, boost future earnings and strengthen an economy. The chapter concludes by outlining some of the flaws in our current knowledge. In particular, we question some of the notions put forward regarding economic returns, arguing that decisions should not be built on the foundations of inadequate evidence and belief-based policy. We also discuss some potential sources of funds (some non-traditional) that theoretically may support long-term investment in human capital development.

Economic insights

Human capital theory

Human capital theory is a useful unifying framework that embraces the complexity of early childhood policy. The theory is underpinned by the notion that individuals and society gain benefits from investing in people (Sweetland, 1996). It proposes that: (1) later skills build on earlier skills; (2) development occurs over multiple stages of the life course; (3) human development involves the interaction of nature and nurture; and (4) human capital, skills and capabilities are multidimensional (Kilburn & Karoly, 2008; Manning, 2008). The word investment, in this context, differentiates human capital expenditures from consumption expenditures, the latter providing few benefits beyond immediate gratification (Vaizey, 1962). Although it is widely acknowledged that human capital investment includes the domains of health and nutrition (Schultz, 1982), education consistently emerges as the empirical frontrunner. The primary reason for this is that education is perceived, by society at large, to contribute to health and nutritional improvements (Schultz, 1963). In addition, and probably an important empirical reason is that education can be measured in quantitative terms (e.g. dollars and years) (Checchi, 2006).

The theory proposes that the benefits derived from investment in early education are diverse. As well as contributing to an individual's health and nutrition, education tends to effect a control on population growth and overall quality of life (Becker, 1993). Education is also a conduit to citizenry enlightenment and engagement. Education is seen to provide the skills necessary to participate in democratic and legal due process. In addition, it provides an avenue to pursue values such as equality, fraternity and liberty at individual and social levels (Swanson & King, 1991).

Human capital theory tends to be consistent with developmental outcome patterns captured in empirical analyses of early childhood education and skills development programs. For example, policies that attempt to increase the education level of parents (particularly mothers) and caregivers show the unique predictive role of enhanced parental education on their children's future development, underscoring the importance of mediators of parental education effects (e.g. achievement-related aspirations) (Dubow, Boxer & Huesmann, 2009). Early childhood education and skills development programs underpinned by human capital theory tend to be more effective on related outcomes (e.g. reductions in special education placement and grade retention) if implemented in the preschool years as opposed to later, for example, in primary school (Manning, Homel, & Smith, 2010; Reynolds et al., 2002). Finally, the early health screening (including mental health) of children mediates future problems and promotes

64 Economics perspectives in Australia

healthy development and transitions along positive developmental pathways. For example, research suggests that children in foster care are at higher risk of developing, or in fact having, mental health problems than those who are not (Kortenkamp, 2002). Understandably, a compelling argument can be made for the early provision of mental health screening and services particularly when evidence suggests that mental health problems can be identified in early childhood (Egger & Angold, 2006; Zeanah & Zeanah, 2009) and the early provision of services helps reduce emotional disorders in later life (young adulthood) (Nelson et al., 2003). Specifically, the universal promotion of mental health awareness and the funding of effective prevention programs used to promote wellbeing prior to problem behaviours becoming observable or problematic (for those who already have early symptoms of mental health difficulties) is a social justice and economic imperative. Should such problems be unobserved or left untreated, a range of poor immediate and future outcomes, including lower school performance (Tremblay et al., 1992) will inevitably prevail.

Economic return on investment

As well as being underpinned by Human Capital theory, a growing body of program evaluations shows that early childhood education and skills development programs produce a range of returns to individuals, government and society at large. Table 4.1 provides an illustration of some the potential benefits that may be produced by such programs.

Much has also been documented regarding the potential economic return on investment. For example, Heckman et al. (2010b) estimate that the Perry Preschool program (Coalition for evidence-based policy, 2005) yielded returns of between seven and 10 per cent per year based on increased school and career achievement and savings in remedial education, health and criminal justice

Table 4.1 The Benefits of Early Childhood Education and Skills Development

Health	Education	Economic
• Reduced child maltreatment	• Reduced grade repetition	• Increased labour force participation
• Reduced child accidents and injuries	• Reduced use of special education	• Increased adult earnings
• Reduced incidence of teenage pregnancy	• Increased rate of high school graduation	• Reduced welfare transfer payments
• Reduced incidence of smoking and illicit substance abuse	• Increased rate of high school students transitioning to postsecondary education	• Increased tax base
• Improved pregnancy outcomes		• Reduced criminal justice expenditures

Adapted from Karoly, Kilburn, and Cannon (2005)

expenditures. In another example, the economic analysis of the Chicago Child-Parent Center study undertaken by Reynolds et al. (2002) estimated that the program yielded a net return to society of US$7.14 (present value 1998 dollars). This return was attributed to increased economic wellbeing and tax revenues and savings derived from reductions in public expenditures for remedial education, criminal justice treatment and crime victims. The extended program (four to six years' participation) yielded returns of approximately six dollars per dollar invested and $1.66 per dollar invested for the school-age program. Table 4.2 provides a selection of economic analyses conducted of early childhood education and skills development programs. The table displays the age at last follow-up for each program, program costs, total program benefits, net program benefits (i.e. benefits minus costs) and the cost-benefit ratio for each program, calculated by dividing total program benefits by program costs.

While the program had significant and favorable effects as of the last follow-up at age eight, none of the outcomes assessed could be translated into dollar savings. The important insight we have gained from these economic analyses is that results often differ. For example, not all programs produce benefits that offset their costs. Kilburn and Karoly (2008) find that approximately 75 per cent of economic analyses undertaken in this field produce benefit-cost ratios greater than 1 (i.e. benefits outweigh the costs). However, the answer regarding return on investment may differ when viewed from the government's perspective. This means that not all programs generate sufficient net savings (even though the program produces positive net benefits to society as a whole) to offset public sector investment. Second, there is wide variation in benefit-cost ratios. These variations are, typically, due to differences in the length of follow-up for the program evaluations and the range of outcomes measured. For example, those programs with high cost-benefit ratios (e.g. Perry Preschool Project and Chicago CPC) have longer follow-up times (e.g. to age 21 or 40). In addition, some programs produced no net benefits. CCDP, for example, found no significant improvements in measurable outcomes, while IHDP (although producing favorable results) could not readily express outcomes in dollar terms. Third, results reveal a large variation with respect to payoffs. Variation is often found between the scale (i.e. small-scale (model) programs vs. larger-scale programs), cost (i.e. expensive and less expensive) and format (i.e. centre-based vs. in the home) of programs. Finally, there is evidence that returns dissipate under certain conditions. Less targeted programs, for example, are more fragile in this respect compared to targeted programs (Kilburn & Karoly, 2008).

Digging a little deeper

Investing in young children, particularly in centers of education and care, has the potential to reduce social and economic inequality. The bottom line is that our early years of life are largely shaped by things we can't control, for example: others around us (e.g. parents, siblings), the environment we live in, educational

Table 4.2 Economic Benefits of Selected Early Childhood Education and Skills Development Programs

Program	Author	Goals	Age at Last Follow-up	Program Costs ($)	Total Benefits to Society ($)	Net Benefits ($)	Benefit-Cost Ratio
High/Scope Perry Preschool Project	Belfiled et al. (2006)	Improve intellectual and social development of young children	40	14,830	253,154	238,324	17.07
Abecedarian Program	Masse and Barnett (2002)	Determine whether early childhood education can prevent retarded development of high-risk children	21	42,871	138,635	95,764	3.23
Chicago CPC	Reynolds et al. (2002)	Promote cognitive and socio-emotional development to prepare child for school entry and beyond	21	6,913	49,337	42,424	7.14
Home Instruction Program for Preschool Youngsters (HIPPY) USA	Aos et al. (2004)	Help parents with limited education prepare their children for school entry	6	1,681	3,032	1,351	1.80

Infant Health and Development Program (IHDP)*	Aos et al. (2004)	Reduce developmental, behavioral and other health problems	8	49,021	–	–49,021	–
ECE for low-income Three- and four-year-olds	Aos et al., (2004)	Meta-analysis of early childhood education programs	Varies	6,681	15,742	9,061	2.36

Note: All dollar values are 2003 US dollars per child and reflect the present value of amounts over time, where future values are discounted using a 3 per cent annual real discount rate.

68 Economics perspectives in Australia

and economic resources available to us, our genetic makeup and health status, to name a few. These endowments, in part, shape our future lives. What needs to be acknowledged is that our lives are not necessarily set on a linear pathway without any possibility of altering our current trajectory. Homel (2005) rather eloquently states:

> People are not like rockets whose trajectory is established at the moment they are launched. Indeed, it is the lifelong capacity for change and reorganization that renders human beings capable of dramatic recovery from early harm and incapable of being inoculated against later adversity. This lifelong plasticity renders us both adaptive and vulnerable
>
> (p. 71).

In saying this, however, Elder (1998) acknowledged that:

> But not even great talent and industry can ensure life success over adversity without opportunity . . . Generations of young Chinese also learned this during the Cultural Revolution when important life decisions were made by the work unit, and many thousands were sent down from the city to the rural countryside and mines. Members of this "sent-down generation" were disadvantaged in education, work careers, mate selection, and family formation
>
> (p. 9).

The point is, that even though we have the capacity to change, we must not blindly assume that this change will occur organically, without external assistance. With this assistance, our potential to succeed and live rich, meaningful and satisfying lives is greatly enhanced.

Underpinned by Human Capital theory and supported by empirical evidence, many economists believe this to be the case; they argue that human capital investment has the potential, among other things, to improve health outcomes, boost future earnings and strengthen our economy.

Timing of investment is also an important element, with Heckman (2006) proposing that the earlier the investment, the greater the return. Heckman argues that programs or services delivered to disadvantaged children in the early years of life significantly enhance the rate of return to investment in human capital. He also proposes that, at existing funding levels, we overinvest in the later years of schooling and underinvest in the preschool years. Further, as we age, the rate of return declines.

Evidence of improved health outcomes

Most policies that focus on combatting disease, disorder, morbidity and illness (terms often used interchangeably)[1] focus on treatment in the adult years, once the disease is presented.

Governments who try to control the soaring costs of a health care system often emphasise tertiary prevention. That is, attempting to control what are often escalating health problems in people who are already ill. There is, however, a complementary approach, which involves preventing disease or delaying its onset. This appears to be a promising, moreover wise, strategy given that adult illnesses tend to be more prevalent and challenging among those who are exposed to adversity in early life (Danese et al., 2007; Galobardes, Lynch, & Smith, 2008).

In the recent past it was assumed that education mediates health. However, more recent evidence suggests that early health and nutrition coupled with early education provide the necessary ingredients for better adult health (Campbell et al., 2014). The mechanisms through which experiences in early life shape our later life health are being investigated (Entringer, Buss, & Wadhwa, 2012; Hertzman, 1999), however, empirical evidence remains limited. Irrespective, there are longitudinal studies that demonstrate that providing intensive and focused intervention in the early years (e.g. preschool) can be effective in preventing, and in some cases, delaying the onset of later adult disease. The Carolina Abecedarian Project (ABC) (Campbell et al., 2002b) was one such program that allowed researchers to test this link.

The ABC program tested whether an intellectually stimulating early childhood environment could reduce developmental delays among an at-risk community of children in Chapel Hill, North Carolina. The study consisted of two stages of treatment. Stage one (preschool stage) began soon after birth and continued until the child was five years of age. Stage two (school-age stage) started when the child was six years of age and concluded at age eight. The program also included nutritional and health components where children received two healthy meals and an afternoon snack. In addition, the project offered parents the opportunity for their child to be periodically examined by a medical expert with additional daily health screenings. Stage one involved periods of cognitive and social stimulation (e.g. language development, emotional regulation and cognitive skills) (see for example, Sparling & Lewis, 1979) combined with caregiving and supervised play. Stage two focused on cultivating early math and reading skills development.

Campbell et al. (2014), using recently collected biomedical data on both treatment and control groups (stage one randomisation) of the ABC participants, attempted to examine whether the program produced long-term health improvements. In summary, their analysis demonstrates long-term statistically significant differences between the treatment and control groups at age 35 (Table 4.3).

In summary, in terms of the prevention of chronic diseases such as hypertension, heart disease, diabetes and obesity, both males and females in the treatment group had a significantly lower prevalence of risk factors for cardiovascular and metabolic disease. Males were found to have lower systolic and diastolic blood pressure and were less likely to fall into the stage 1 hypertension category, while females were less likely to fall into the pre-hypertension category. Control males were twice as likely to be affected by vitamin D deficiency. In terms of improved adult physical health, males had significantly higher levels of "good" HDL

70 Economics perspectives in Australia

Table 4.3 Health Effects of the Carolina Abecedarian Project (Age 35)

Variable	Control mean	Treatment mean	Mean difference	Conditional treatment effect	Treatment p-value
Diastolic blood pressure (mm Hg)	92.000	78.526	13.474	19.220	0.024
Systolic blood pressure (mm Hg)	143.333	125.789	17.544	24.828	0.018
Hypertension (systolic bp ≥ 140 and diastolic bp ≥ 90	0.444	0.105	0.339	0.537	0.010
High Density Lipoprotein (HDL) Cholesterol (mg/dL)	42.000	53.211	11.211	11.720	0.066
Vitamin D deficiency (<20 ng/mL)	0.750	0.368	0.382	0.435	0.021
Severely obese (BMI ≥ 35)	0.375	0.111	0.264	0.404	0.115
Abnormal obesity (WHR > 0.9)	0.875	0.647	0.228	0.294	0.137
Metabolic syndrome (NCEP definition)	0.250	0.000	0.250	0.465	0.007

Adapted from Campbell et al. (2014)

Note: A conditional treatment effect is the average effect of treatment on the individual. This is different to a marginal treatment effect, where the effect relates to the average effect of treatment on the population.[2]

cholesterol, while females were less likely to be affected by abnormal obesity. Males in the control group had metabolic syndrome. This syndrome dramatically increases the risk of heart disease, stroke and diabetes. In terms of increases in healthy behaviours, females were less likely to start drinking before the age of 17, more likely to engage in physical activity and more likely to eat nutritious food. Males delayed the onset of smoking and marijuana use (Campbell et al., 2014).

A review of the causal effect of education on health and health-related behaviours of children of the British Cohort Study (Conti, Heckman, & Urzua, 2010) revealed that early health and development are equally as important as education in promoting increased employment prospects, enhanced productivity, higher earning capacity, upward mobility and better health in the future. The authors developed an empirical model of schooling choice and post-schooling outcomes where both outcomes are influenced by the family environment and latent capabilities (cognitive, non-cognitive and health). The authors find a weak link between early health and education (as emphasised by Currie (2008)) and instead find that early health has a statistically significant direct effect on adult outcomes whereby non-cognitive factors play an important role in predicting healthy behaviours. Notably, education is found to have a strong causal effect on most outcomes. Interestingly though, education plays a more important causal role for males with respect to rates of obesity, exercise and employment. Although there is a significant amount of heterogeneity in the effects of education across outcomes by levels of endowment, specific patterns emerge. For males, " . . . the positive effects of education are much larger at the bottom of the non-cognitive ability distribution and at the top of the cognitive ability distribution" (p. 4).

Evidence of boosting future earnings

The evidence regarding the long-term economic benefits of early development interventions, targeted at a time when brain plasticity and neurogenesis are high (thus an important period for cognitive and psychosocial skill development), is substantial (Aughinbaugh, 2001; Campbell et al., 2002a, 2012, 2014; Garces, Thomas, & Currie, 2000; Heckman et al., 2010a, 2010b; Reynolds, Ou, & Topitzes, 2004; Reynolds et al., 2007, 2011). In short, at least in the U.S., early childhood interventions produce long-term economic benefits. These benefits are typically distributed in the long term with respect to employment effects on: (1) former early childhood program participants; (2) increased education or labour supply of parents; and (3) stimulation of the state economy (Bartik, 2013).

In regards to (1), early childhood programs typically increase the probability of achieving a higher level of education, which leads to improved job skills, the chances of getting a higher paid, more secure job, and for the economy, a higher-quality labour force to draw from leading to higher local per capita earnings. In terms of (2), parents or caregivers who have access to stable, high-quality childcare/early education are able to improve their productivity in terms of labour force participation, work more hours, take less days off work, reduce their levels of stress due to trying to manage work with their parental caring responsibilities and/or pursuing education. What should be noted is that early childhood programs positively affect the labour supply, but the effects of the program are typically greater for children than for parents. However, programs that target families and the issues they face (e.g. caring responsibilities) produce larger effects on parents. Finally, focusing on (3), government spending on early childhood programs appear to produce multiplier effects. For example, local programs will buy local goods and services, employees of these programs will buy local goods and services etc. These multiplier effects are politically appealing as the benefits are derived almost immediately. What should be noted is that government investment in early childhood programs requires a funding stream. This funding may be obtained by increasing taxes. But, it may also come from local investment through non-for-profit agencies or non-government organizations (Bartik, 2013). We discuss, in detail, potential funding options at the end of the chapter. The real question is what multiplier effects are left once one accounts for taxes and spending. Although the net benefits may be modest, they may still be positive. More research is required to fully examine this question.

So what is the expected return on investment for an economy? Drawing from the work of Bartik (2013), each dollar invested in a high-quality early childhood program will return between US $2 to $3 to a state economy (i.e. earnings per capita of state residents). Bartik estimated the returns on investment derived for three programs: (1) a universal pre-kindergarten program, which was modelled after the Chicago Child-Parent Center (Reynolds et al., 2002; Temple & Reynolds, 2007) and the Perry Preschool Program (Schweinhart et al., 2005). This program offered free pre-kindergarten education to all four-year-old children for three hours per day over the schooling year; (2) the Abecedarian Program, a targeted program where disadvantaged and high-risk families (e.g. single parent, low income, low education) received five years of free full-time (7.30am to 5.30pm, five days a week) childcare and pre-kindergarten education for 50 weeks of the year (Ramey & Campbell, 1991); and (3) the Nurse Family Partnership Program, which provided first-time mothers from disadvantaged backgrounds 30 nurse home visits, beginning before the child was born (average of seven visits) until their child turned two years of age (average of 23 visits) (Olds, 2002; Olds, Kitzman, et al., 2004; Olds, Robinson, et al., 2004). Respectively, the three programs produced benefits of US $2.78, $2.25 and $1.85 per dollar invested. The estimated benefits to the state did not include benefits to participants who moved out of the state or benefits from reduced crime. The sizes of the respective programs' effects on a state economy differ dramatically due to scale differences across programs. Bartik (2013) estimated that should a state adopt a full-scale Abecedarian program, present value of residents' earnings would increase by about 1.7 per cent. The full-scale adoption of the universal pre-kindergarten program would increase residents' earnings by about 0.75 per cent and the full-scale adoption of the Nurse Family Partnership Program would increase residents' earnings by about 0.1 per cent. In the long term such increases would amount to a conservative estimate of hundreds of billions of dollars.

Few studies examining the economic benefits derived from early childhood interventions, however, have been conducted in developing nations with most data primarily U.S.-based. One exception is the study conducted by Gertler et al. (2014b). The study examined the causal effects of an intervention that gave psychosocial stimulation to growth-stunted Jamaican toddlers on future earnings. The authors found that program participants, similar to home visiting programs in the United States, had significantly increased earnings in adulthood. This result put their wages on par with those of their more advantaged peers. Table 4.4 reports the estimated impacts of treatment on log monthly earnings for the observed sample. This includes imputations for the earnings of nine missing migrants. Results show that the intervention produced a statistically significant effect on future earnings, where the average earnings of the treatment group are 25 per cent higher compared to the control group. "Treatments effects are interpreted as the differences in the means of log earnings [between the treated and control groups] conditional on baseline values of child age, gender, weight-for-height z-score and maternal education" (p. 999). P-values represent one-sided block permutation tests of the null hypothesis (single P-value in parentheses) of no treatment effect and multiple hypotheses (step-down P-value in brackets) of no treatment. In the last column, a combined statistic is used to summarize participant outcomes. Ninety-eight per cent of children in the treatment group were employed at age 22, with 94 per cent of them in full-time employment. In addition to future earnings, the intervention narrowed the achievement gap and reduced inequality in later life. The authors argue that "The program may have improved children's skills to the point where families were encouraged to seek greater education and employment opportunities" (Gertler et al., 2014a, p. 2).

Strengthen an economy

Heckman (2015a) states "the rate of return for investments in quality early childhood development for disadvantaged children is 7–10 per cent per annum through better outcomes in education, health, sociability, economic productivity and reduced crime" (p. 2). This statement, conceptually, seems plausible as children who grow up in unfavourable environments are faced with deficits in skills and abilities that inevitably adversely impact on individual productivity and increase social costs, which ultimately are borne by society in terms of financial deficits.

Table 4.4 Treatment Effect on Average Log Earnings at Age 22

Job	All job types	Full-time jobs only	Non-temporary jobs	Rank mean
Treatment effect	0.30	0.22	0.39	0.09
Single P-value	(0.01)	(0.04)	(0.01)	(0.04)
Step-down P-value	[0.02]	[0.04]	[0.02]	–
Control mean	9.40	9.59	9.67	0.36

Adapted from Gertler et al. (2014b)

In principle, to strengthen an economy and reduce deficits we need to invest in programs that produce greater returns in education, health and productivity. In short, the consensus among most academics is to invest in human capital in order to strengthen the economy and reduce deficits. James Heckman, a strong advocate of such investment, proposes that we specifically focus on:

1 Prioritizing investment in quality early childhood education for at-risk children – In the absence of such investment (i.e. parent training and quality early education programs) many at-risk children and their families will miss the developmental growth that is of fundamental importance to their future success. Once behind, it is difficult (but not impossible) to catch up with mainstream society. Ultimately, if this deficiency is not addressed a price will be paid in terms of higher social costs and declining economic prosperity.
2 Developing cognitive and character skills early – Skills such as attentiveness, impulse control, persistence, the inhibition of aggressive reactions and working collaboratively are fundamental to educational, career and life success. Such skills need to be mastered early to ensure that an individual is not left behind educationally, or worse, isolated by peers due to antisocial behaviours.
3 Providing developmental resources to children and their families – Directing resources to the children alone is not enough. It needs to be complemented by investment in parents and families. This would include, for example, home visiting programs for parents such as the Prenatal and Early Childhood Nurse Home Visitation Program (Olds, Kitzman, et al., 2004), which is designed to help low-income, first-time parents begin their lives with their children on a positive note in order to prevent health and parenting problems that may manifest into, or contribute to, the early development of antisocial behavioral problems.

According to Heckman (2015b) those seeking to reduce deficits and strengthen the economy should invest in early childhood education. The returns to investing in early education are upward mobility and building a highly educated, skilled workforce, which in turn, are the necessary ingredients to strengthening an economy. In terms of deficit reduction, this will only come about through the careful investment of public and private dollars. Data show that an incredibly effective strategy for promoting economic growth is investing in the development of human capital. Hanushek (2013) states, "without improving school quality, developing countries will find it difficult to improve their long run economic performance" (p. 204). The short-term costs associated with this investment can potentially reduce the need for special and remedial education, which has been demonstrated to be incredibly expensive compared to investing early (Manning, 2004; Manning, Homel, & Smith., 2006), better health outcomes (Campbell et al., 2014), a reduced need for social services (Manning, 2008), lower criminal justice costs (Manning et al., 2010) and increased self-sufficiency and productivity in the family (Duncan, Kalil, & Ziol-Guest, 2015; Sanders, 2003; Sanders, Markie-Dadds, & Turner, 2003).

Issues of causation

A question that consistently arises is 'what are the real causal pathways'? The answer to this question is fundamental in ensuring that policy is not just belief-based. The analytical concern regarding the relationship between human capital investment and economic growth is that the growth relationships do not accurately measure causal influences. Rather, they reflect reverse causation, omitted variable bias, cultural differences, etcetera. This concern is central to the interpretation of much empirical analysis in this area. As an example, countries that develop faster have the resources to invest in high-quality early education. This investment could result in, for example, higher test scores in children who reside in countries who have the resources to heavily invest. Although there are studies that have begun to examine this notion (Hanushek & Woessmann, 2010), further exploration of quasi-experimental settings in the international data should be of paramount importance. In short, with limited international variations, it is extremely difficult to demonstrate, conclusively, a real causal relationship between human capital investment and economic growth. This is not to say that it does not exist. Rather, more funded research is required to examine the relationship.

Fragile estimates

Much of the economic case for expanding preschool education, particularly for children from disadvantaged backgrounds, is based on evidence from the High-Scope Perry Preschool Program (Belfield et al., 2006). Critics (see for example, Hanushek & Lindseth, 2009), not necessarily of the program but certainly of the strength of evidence, argue that small sample size (n=123 children – 58 randomly assigned to receive the program and 65 in a control group), lack of long-term treatment effects on IQ and the absence of statistical significance for a number of estimated treatment effects render the Perry estimates particularly fragile. Estimates, for example, have been cited in the range of 16 (Rolnick & Grunewald, 2003) and 17 (Belfield et al., 2006) per cent rate of return. As stated by Heckman et al. (2010b), "All of the reported estimates of rates of return are presented without standard errors leaving readers uncertain as to whether the estimates are statistically significantly different from zero" (pp. 114–115). As an example, the study conducted by Rolnick and Grunewald (2003) does not conduct sensitivity analyses for the effects of alternative assumptions. Nor does it produce standard errors for the estimated rates of return. Similarly, Belfield et al. (2006) does not report standard errors, although the authors do conduct a limited sensitivity analysis.

In an attempt to overcome a series of limitations presented by earlier Perry Preschool Program studies, Heckman et al. (2010b) re-estimates the rate of return and benefit-to-cost ratio for the program. Building on the cost-benefit analyses conducted by Barnett (1985) and Barnett (1996), the authors derive more robust results by: (1) accounting for compromised randomisation due to the re-assignment of treatment and controls after randomisation and some imbalance in baseline variables between treatment and control groups – the authors correct for these problems using matching as outlined in Heckman et al. (2009); (2) developing standard errors where possible for estimates of the rate of return and benefit-cost ratios; (3) examine the sensitivity of estimates of rates of return where standard errors could not be determined; (4) adjust for the deadweight costs of taxation, that is dollars of welfare loss per tax dollar; (5) employ a wider variety of methods to impute within-sample missing earnings than have been used in the previous literature and examine the sensitivity of estimates; (6) extrapolate missing future earnings for both treatment and control group participants and examine the sensitivity of estimates; and (7) employ local data on costs of education, crime and welfare participation rather than using national-level data.

Heckman et al. (2010b) estimate that the overall social rate of return to the Perry Preschool Program ranges from 7–10 per cent. Heckman and colleagues state:

> Annual rates of return of this magnitude, if compounded and reinvested annually over a 65-year life, imply that each dollar invested at age 4 yields a return of 60–300 dollars by age 65. Stated another way, the benefit-cost ratio for the Perry program, accounting for deadweight costs of taxes and assuming a 3% discount rate, ranges from 7 to 12 dollars per person, i.e., each dollar invested returns in present value terms 7 to 12 dollars back to society
>
> (pp. 115–116).

Estimates are presented below in Table 4.5. The main difference between Heckman and colleagues' estimates and those of previous studies lies in the way they evaluate the social cost of crime. In short, Heckman and colleagues' estimation is much lower because they assume that there are no victim costs associated with driving 'misdemeanours' and drug-related crimes. This is important as these costs represent a significant proportion of overall benefits derived from the program.

Although Heckman and colleagues have produced more reliable and robust estimates of the rate of return and benefit-to-cost ratios of the Perry Preschool Program, this does not mean that all programs of this nature will produce similar results. Enough studies in this area have demonstrated the fragility of programs to changes in key variables. In short, one must always question generalizability and transferability. As an example, the Elmira Nurse Home Visitation Program did not produce consistent results when moved between areas (e.g. Memphis and Denver), when delivered to mothers from different backgrounds, or when changes were made with regards to program delivery by trained nurses and para-professionals. Although initial analyses indicate that the program remains effective across racial, ethnic, geographic and socio-economic groups, one cannot assume that the economic returns are indeed similar. In this frame, context matters.

Table 4.5 Selected Estimates of Internal Rates of Return (%) and Benefit-to-Cost Ratios

Murder cost[b]		To the individual			To society[a]			To society[a]		
					High ($4.1 Million)			Low ($13,000)		
		All[d]	Male	Female	All[d]	Male	Female	All[d]	Male	Female
	Deadweight loss[c]									
IRR	0%	7.6	8.4	7.8	9.9	11.4	17.1	9	12.2	9.8
		(1.8)	(1.7)	(1.1)	(4.1)	(3.4)	(4.9)	(3.5)	(3.1)	(1.8)
	50%	6.2	6.8	6.8	9.2	10.7	14.9	8.1	11.1	8.1
		(1.2)	(1.1)	(1.0)	(2.9)	(3.2)	(4.8)	(2.6)	(3.1)	(1.7)
	100%	5.3	5.9	5.7	8.7	10.2	13.6	7.6	10.4	7.5
		(1.1)	(1.1)	(0.9)	(2.5)	(3.1)	(4.9)	(2.4)	(2.9)	(1.8)
	Discount rate									
Benefit-cost ratios	0%				31.5	33.7	27.0	19.1	22.8	12.7
					(11.3)	(17.3)	(14.4)	(5.4)	(8.3)	(3.8)
	3%				12.2	12.1	11.6	7.1	8.6	4.5
					(5.3)	(8.0)	(7.1)	(2.3)	(3.7)	(1.4)
	5%				6.8	6.2	7.1	3.9	4.7	2.4
					(3.4)	(5.1)	(4.6)	(1.5)	(2.3)	(0.8)
	7%				3.9	3.2	4.6	2.2	2.7	1.4
					(2.3)	(3.4)	(3.1)	(0.9)	(1.5)	(0.5)

Adapted from Heckman et al. (2010)

[a] The sum of returns to program participants and the general public.
[b] High murder cost accounts for the standard statistical value of life, while low does not.
[c] Deadweight cost is dollars of welfare loss per tax dollar.
[d] All is computed from an average of the profiles of the pooled sample, and may be lower or higher than the profiles for each gender group.
Note 1: Parentheses represent standard errors. Standard errors were calculated by Heckman et al. (2010) by Monte Carlo resampling of prediction errors and bootstrapping.

Note 2: Kernel matching using NLSY data was used to impute missing values for earnings before age-40. PSID projection was used for extrapolation of later earnings.

Note 3: In calculating benefit-to-cost ratios, the deadweight loss of taxation was assumed to be 50 per cent.

Note 4: Nine types of crime are used to estimate the social cost of crime (see http://jenni.uchicago.edu/Perry/Rate-of-Return-apx-2009–11–23b_cji.pdf).

Potential investment opportunities

So how can we support the required level of investment in human capital development programs (e.g. fully funded preschool education and parental support services) when government budgets are straining to meet current demands? In short, we need to become a little more creative. A number of non-traditional alternative funding sources exist. Economists are well placed to provide advice on these sources given their success in other areas of social and environmental investment. In addition to state and commonwealth funding opportunities, it is also envisaged that future funding in human capital investment will be increasingly sought from private investments and philanthropic contributions. We discuss these potential sources below.

Private equity investment

Private equity is an asset class consisting of equity securities and debt in operating companies that are not publicly traded on a stock exchange. A private equity investment will generally be made by a private equity firm, a venture capital firm or an angel investor. Each of these categories of investor has its own set of goals, preferences and investment strategies; however, all provide working capital to a target company or organisation.

In recent years, there has been a significant shift in investor attitude towards making socially and environmentally responsible investments, as well as divesting from socially and environmentally harmful investments (e.g. fossil fuels, tobacco and gambling). However, there are questions around the ability of government-run programs to acquire private equity investment. This issue would need to be carefully considered when seeking this source of funding.

Responsible investment

Responsible investment is an umbrella term used to describe an investment process that takes environmental, social, governance (ESG) or ethical considerations into account. Responsible investing is any investment strategy that seeks to consider both financial return and social good. In general, socially responsible investors encourage corporate practices that promote environmental stewardship, consumer protection, human rights and diversity. Some avoid businesses involved in alcohol, tobacco, gambling, pornography, weapons, fossil fuel production and/or the military.

The peak industry body representing responsible and ethical investors across Australia and New Zealand is the Responsible Investment Association Australasia. The body has over 150 members who have in excess of AUD $500 billion in assets under management. Members include some of Australia's largest and most well-known financial services companies. Fund manager members include AMP Capital, BT Investment Management, Perpetual and Colonial First State Global Asset Management. Superannuation fund members include UniSuper, Hesta and Sunsuper.

Superannuation funds

Australian superannuation funds are significant contributors to responsible investment flows in Australia, through the practice of incorporating environmental, social and corporate governance practices into their business (such as becoming signatories of the United Nations Principles of Responsible Investment) or through offering responsible investment options to their clients. Analysis

Economics perspectives in Australia   79

conducted by the Responsible Investment Association Australasia (2014) indicates that approximately one-quarter of the largest 100 superannuation funds in Australia offer socially responsible investment options to their clients. As an example of dollars invested, the five highest-ranking Australian superannuation funds, which include Australian Ethical, VicSuper, Christian Super, Unisuper and Local Government Super have a total of approximately AUD $8.0 billion invested under a core responsible investment strategy.

Philanthropic investment

The most promising, and potentially easiest strategy to negotiate is philanthropic funding. Philanthropy can be defined as the planned and structured giving of money, time, information, goods and services, voice and influence to improve the wellbeing of humanity and the community. This normally involves trusts, foundations, organizations, families and individuals who engage in philanthropic activities (Philanthropy Australia, 2013).

Philanthropic donations by individuals and businesses are a potential source of funding for human capital investment projects. As organizations become more attuned to corporate social responsibility issues, and as investors increasingly value corporate social responsibility, opportunities for philanthropic funding options are likely to increase.

The lack of mandatory reporting makes it impossible to give accurate data, but Philanthropy Australia (2014) estimates that there are approximately 5,000 foundations in Australia giving between AUD $0.5 billion to $1 billion annually. This includes almost 3,000 Private and Public Ancillary Funds, and approximately 2,000 charitable trusts and foundations administered by trustee companies. Table 4.6 shows the top 10 philanthropic foundations in Australia and their level of funding.

According to the 2014 Australian Giving Trends report (McLeod, 2014), giving has remained flat since the global financial crisis. Nonetheless, the long-term

Table 4.6 Ten Largest Philanthropic Foundations in Australia, 2010–11

Name	Disbursement (AUD) $ million)
Macquarie Group Foundation	17.7
The Ian Potter Foundation	12.4
The Sidney Myer Fund and The Myer Foundation	11
Lord Mayor's Charitable Foundation	7.7
Geoffrey Gardiner Dairy Foundation	7.2
AMP Foundation	6.2 (2010 figures)
Colonial Foundation	5.6
Helen Macpherson Smith Trust	5.5
R. E. Ross Trust	5.3
The William Buckland Foundation	3.3

80 Economics perspectives in Australia

trend is positive with donations rising from AUD $59 million to $2.4 billion per annum between 1979 and 2013, an average annual increase of 11.7 per cent. This increase is largely due to an increase in annual gift size from $31 to $494 per donor. An increasing number of donors has also helped; however, the proportion of people giving has remained relatively flat after peaking in 1983. Volatility in annual giving has increased over the last decade, and the number of charities continues to rise as does the competition for funding.

As stated at the beginning of this section, philanthropy is potentially a very rewarding strategy when it comes to funding opportunities for human capital investment. In 2010, Philanthropy Australia was engaged by the Commonwealth Department of Families, Housing, Community Services and Indigenous Affairs to explore strategies to encourage greater levels of giving among Australia's high and ultra-high net worth individuals (Effective Philanthropy, 2011). The report found that, overall, giving levels as a percentage of Gross Domestic Product are slightly lower in Australia than in the UK and Canada, and that, in general, Australian high and ultra-high net worth individuals tend to give at a relatively low level. These data indicate, however, that overall giving in Australia has increased steadily over the past decade.

The report proposes a number of strategies through which government can increase the level of giving among these individuals. The recommendations fall into two categories: System Recommendations, which cover actions that aim to strengthen the underlying service system supporting the philanthropic sector to better enable and facilitate giving activity; and Program Recommendations, that cover targeted initiatives that aim to increase the number of high and ultra-high net worth individuals involved in giving and increase the amount of money that they give.

The most comprehensive Australian study of philanthropic giving was published by the Australian Government (2007). This report was based on two studies, one by the Bureau of Rural Sciences, which concentrated on incentives for encouraging conservation and environmental philanthropy, and the other by the Commonwealth Scientific and Industrial Research Organisation, which focused on options and attitudes to environmental philanthropy. Although the focus was on the environment, the lessons learnt are nonetheless important. The report identifies various ways in which philanthropy could be encouraged in Australia. These recommendations are broadly applicable to human capital investment and include:

- **Increase awareness** – Creating and maintaining an awareness of social issues. Information and education material focusing on the range of institutions involved, the types of current schemes and the means by which people can become involved would help to increase awareness of human capital philanthropy in Australia, as would developing new policies targeting different groups of stakeholders, such as retiring baby boomers.

Economics perspectives in Australia   81

- **Establish broader categories for human capital philanthropic contributions** – Contributions from the corporate or private sectors could be put towards broader human capital objectives, such as providing access to high-quality early childhood education, family support services and parental educational opportunities (particularly for disadvantaged young mothers) which, as discussed earlier in the chapter, will lead to improved health outcomes for children and their families, social and emotional development, and improved employment outcomes for the child and their parents.
- **Increase involvement of foundations and corporations** – Organisations could, for example, assist in monitoring projects and aligning them more strongly with, for example, regional strategies. They could also help to improve relationships and coordination between local, state and federal governments, in terms of incentives. Better coordination of activities in various jurisdictions might also reduce the complexity of current schemes.
- **Develop more secure and ongoing programs** – Programs could be made more secure by having longer timelines for ensuring that human capital covenants and financing agreements are processed efficiently, and ensuring that governments provide clear and consistent support with coordination across different levels of government.
- **Improve financial incentives** – Ideas include providing stewardship payments to cover management costs for people on lower incomes who need them, and providing a tax rebate to anyone assisting in the current provision of services.
- **Overcome practical barriers** – Options include setting up schemes to recognise and reward contributions, improving access to local labour, and using a facilitator to help individuals and groups to achieve improved outcomes.

In all, it would appear there is some scope for philanthropic investment in human capital investment projects. However, this is likely to be a relatively volatile source of investment, subject to economic fluctuations and the changing priorities of donors.

The way forward

Much of the motivation for human capital investment is founded on the basis that such investment will lead to economic growth that potentially has positive influences on future higher levels of income and living standards. The focus on reducing poverty and economic inequality, in both developed and developing countries, relates directly to economic growth because simply redistributing income will not lead to long-run reduction in poverty or economic inequality (Hanushek, 2013). As discussed in this chapter, much research supports the notion that cross-country differences in economic growth relate to social and cognitive skill development.

Although evidence demonstrates that human capital investment programs, such as the Perry Preschool Program, produce good estimates of return, we cannot assume that results will be similar when key variables, such as location and mode of delivery, are changed. A particularly poignant point is made by David Olds: "A review of other pregnancy and infancy home visitation programs suggest that many do not work" (Olds, 2012, p. 1). This statement is incredibly important as it suggests that we cannot rely on single studies. Rather, our evidence base needs to be deep and wide. Given that much of the economic case for expanding preschool education, particularly for children from disadvantaged backgrounds, is based on evidence from the HighScope Perry Preschool Program, this is concerning. It may suggest that there is a considerable amount of belief-based policy or policy built on insufficient or poor evidence. This does not suggest that we shouldn't invest in quality early education. Rather, high-quality economic analyses, similar to that conducted by Heckman et al. (2010b), should be common. As discussed in the previous section, this requires the support of government, non-government (both profit and non-for-profit) and philanthropic organizations. It also requires that we become a little more creative in the way that we finance this type of investment.

Notes

1 We use the term disease in this context to refer to any condition that impairs the normal functioning of the body, whereby the disease is associated with dysfunctioning of the human body's normal homeostatic process (Saper, Chou, & Elmquist, 2002). We define disorder as a functional abnormality not caused by infectious organisms, which includes metabolic disorders (D'Aversa et al., 2013). Morbidity we define as a diseased state, disability or poor health due to any cause. And infection we define as a condition of being unhealthy in either body or mind, which prevents the normal healthy function of either the body or mind due to, for example, disease.
2 Conditional treatment effect controlling for cohort, number of siblings, mother's IQ and high-risk index at birth, and accounting for attrition using:

IPW. The IPW probabilities are estimated using: prematurity (gestational age < 37 weeks), a dichotomous indicator for not having an exam for illness or injury in the past two years at age 30, Achenbach DSM attention-deficit/hyperactivity (AD/H) problems scale at age 30, and Achenbach substance abuse scale at age 30.

References

Aos, S., Lieb, R., Mayfield, J., Miller, M., & Pennucci, A. (2004). *Benefits and costs of prevention and early intervention programs for youth*. Washington, DC: Washington State Institute for Public Policy.

Aughinbaugh, A. (2001). Does head start yield long-term benefits? *Journal of Human Resources, 36*(4), 641–665.

Australian Government. (2007). *Encouraging environmental philanthropy: Lessons from Australian case studies and interviews*. Canberra, Australia: Department of the Environment and Water Resources.

Barnett, S.W. (1985). *The perry preschool program and its long-term effects: A benefit-cost analysis.* Ypsilanti, MI: High/Scope Educational Research Foundation.

Barnett, S.W. (1996). *Lives in the balance: Benefit-cost analysis of the Perry Preschool program through age 27.* Michigan: High/Scope Press.

Bartik, T. (2013). *Early childhood programs as an economic development tool: Investing early to prepare the future workforce.* Kalamazoo, MI: Upjohn Institute for Employment Research.

Becker, G. (1993). *Human capital: A theoretical and empirical analysis, with special reference to education* (3rd ed.). Chicago, IL: University of Chicago Press.

Belfield, C.R., Nores, M., Barnett, S., & Schweinhart, L.J. (2006). The high/scope perry preschool program cost–benefit analysis using data from the age-40 followup. *Journal of Human Resources, 41*(1), 162–190.

Belfiled, C.R., Milagros, N., Barnett, S.W., & Schweinhart, L.J. (2006). The high/scope perry preschool program: Cost-benefit analysis using data from the age-40 followup. *Journal of Human Resources, 41*(1), 162–190.

Campbell, F., Conti, G., Heckman, J., Moon, S., Pinto, R., Pungello, E., & Pan, Y. (2014). Early childhood investments substantially boost adult health. *Science, 343*(6178), 1478–1485.

Campbell, F., Pungello, E., Burchinal, M., Kainz, K., Pan, Y., Wasik, B., . . . Ramey, C.T. (2012). Adult outcomes as a function of an early childhood educational program: An Abecedarian Project follow-up. *Developmental Psychology, 48*(4), 1033.

Campbell, F., Ramey, C.T., Pungello, E., Sparling, J., & Miller-Johnson, S. (2002a). Early childhood education: Young adult outcomes from the Abecedarian Project. *Applied Developmental Science, 6*(1), 42–57.

Campbell, F.A., Ramey, C.T., Pungello, E., Sparling, J., & Miller-Johnson, S. (2002b). Early childhood education: Young adult outcomes from the Abecedarian Project. *Applied Developmental Science, 6*(1), 42–57.

Checchi, D. (2006). *The economics of education: Human capital, family background and inequality.* Cambridge: Cambridge University Press.

Coalition for evidence-based policy. (2005). *Perry Preschool Project (High quality preschool for children from disadvantaged backgrounds).* Retrieved from http://www.evidencebasedprograms.org/Default.aspx?tabid=32.

Conti, G., Heckman, J., & Urzua, S. (2010). The education-health gradient. *The American Economic Review, 100*(2), 234.

Currie, J. (2008). Healthy, wealthy, and wise: Socioeconomic status, poor health in childhood, and human capital development. *Journal of Economic Literature, 47*(1), 87–122.

D'Aversa, F., Tortora, A., Ianiro, G., Ponziani, F., Annicchiarico, B., & Gasbarrini, A. (2013). Gut microbiota and metabolic syndrome. *Internal and Emergency Medicine, 8*(1), 11–15.

Danese, A., Pariante, C., Caspi, A., Taylor, A., & Poulton, R. (2007). Childhood maltreatment predicts adult inflammation in a life-course study. *Proceedings of the National Academy of Sciences, 104*(4), 1319–1324.

Dubow, E., Boxer, P., & Huesmann, L. (2009). Long-term effects of parents' education on children's educational and occupational success: Mediation by family interactions, child aggression, and teenage aspirations. *Merrill-Palmer Quarterly, 55*(3), 224.

Duncan, G., Kalil, A., & Ziol-Guest, K. (Eds.) (2015). *Health and education in early childhood: Predictors, interventions and policies.* Cambridge: Cambridge University Press.

Effective Philanthropy. (2011). *Strategies for increasing high net worth and ultra-high net worth giving.* Melbourne, Australia.

Egger, H., & Angold, A. (2006). Common emotional and behavioral disorders in preschool children: Presentation, nosology, and epidemiology. *Journal of Child Psychology and Psychiatry, 47*(3–4), 313–337.

Elder, G. (1998). The life course as developmental theory. *Child Development, 69*(1), 1–12.

Entringer, S., Buss, C., & Wadhwa, P. (2012). Prenatal stress, telomere biology, and fetal programming of health and disease risk. *Science Signaling, 5*(248), pt12–pt12.

Galobardes, B., Lynch, J., & Smith, G. (2008). Is the association between childhood socioeconomic circumstances and cause-specific mortality established? Update of a systematic review. *Journal of Epidemiology and Community Health, 62*(5), 387–390.

Garces, E., Thomas, D., & Currie, J. (2000). Longer-term effects of head start. *American Economic Review, 92*(4), 999–1012.

Gertler, P., Heckman, J., Pinto, R., Zanolini, A., Vermeersch, C., Walker, S., . . . Grantham-McGregor, S. (2014a). *The Jamaican study: Early childhood education can compensate for developmental delays, boost earnings and reduce inequality.* Retrieved from http://heckmanequation.org/content/resource/research-summary-jamaican-study.

Gertler, P., Heckman, J., Pinto, R., Zanolini, A., Vermeersch, C., Walker, S., . . . Grantham-McGregor, S. (2014b). Labor market returns to an early childhood stimulation intervention in Jamaica. *Science, 344*(6187), 998–1001.

Hanushek, E. (2013). Economic growth in developing countries: The role of human capital. *Economics of Education Review, 37*(1), 204–212.

Hanushek, E., & Lindseth, A. (2009). *Schoolhouses, courthouses, and statehouses: Solving the funding-achievement puzzle in America's public schools.* Princeton, NJ: Princeton University Press.

Hanushek, E., & Woessmann, L. (2010). *The economics of international differences in educational achievement.* Cambridge, MA: National Bureau of Economic Research.

Heckman, J.J. (2006). Skill formation and the economics of investing in disadvantaged children. *Science, 312*(5782), 1900–1902.

Heckman, J.J. (2015a). *4 Big benefits of investing in early childhood development.* Retrieved from http://heckmanequation.org/content/4-big-benefits-investing-early-childhood-development.

Heckman, J.J. (2015b). *Invest in early childhood development: Reduce deficits, strengthen the economy.* Retrieved from http://heckmanequation.org/content/resource/invest-early-childhood-development-reduce-deficits-strengthen-economy.

Heckman, J.J., Moon, S., Pinto, R., Savelyev, P., & Yavitz, A. (2009). *A reanalysis of the highscope perry preschool program.* Unpublished manuscript. Department of Economics. Chicago, IL: University of Chicago.

Heckman, J.J., Moon, S., Pinto, R., Savelyev, P., & Yavitz, A. (2010a). Analyzing social experiments as implemented: A reexamination of the evidence from the HighScope Perry Preschool Program. *Quantitative Economics, 1*(1), 1–46.

Heckman, J.J., Moon, S., Pinto, R., Savelyev, P., & Yavitz, A. (2010b). The rate of return to the HighScope Perry Preschool Program. *Journal of Public Economics, 94*(1), 114–128.

Hertzman, C. (1999). The biological embedding of early experience and its effects on health in adulthood. *Annals of the New York Academy of Sciences, 896*(1), 85–95.

Homel, R. (2005). Developmental crime prevention. In N. Tilley (Ed.), *Handbook of crime prevention and community safety* (pp. 71–106). Cullompton, Devon: Willan Publishing.

Karoly, L., Kilburn, M., & Cannon, J. (2005). *Early childhood interventions: Proven results, future promise.* Santa Monica, CA: RAND.

Kilburn, R., & Karoly, L. (2008). *What does economics tell us about early childhood policy? Research Brief.* Santa Monica, CA: RAND.

Kortenkamp, K. (2002). *The well-being of children involved with the child welfare system: A national overview.* Washington, DC: The Urban Institute.

Manning, M. (2004). *Measuring the costs of community-based developmental prevention programs in Australia.* (Masters (Hons)), Griffith University, Brisbane.

Manning, M. (2008). *Economic evaluation of the effects of early childhood intervention programs on adolescent outcomes.* (PhD), Griffith University, Brisbane.

Manning, M., Homel, R., & Smith, C. (2006). Economic evaluation of a community-based early intervention program implemented in a disadvantaged urban area of Queensland. *Economic Analysis and Policy, 36*(1 & 2), 99–120.

Manning, M., Homel, R., & Smith, C. (2010). A meta-analysis of the effects of early developmental prevention programs in at-risk populations on non-health outcomes in adolescence. *Children and Youth Services Review, 32*(4), 506–519.

Masse, L., & Barnett, S. (2002). Benefit-cost analysis of the Abecedarian early childhood intervention. In H. Levin & P.J. McEwan (Eds.), *Cost-effectiveness and educational policy* (pp. 157–173). Larchmont, NY: Eye on Education, Inc.

McLeod, J. (2014). *Australian giving trends: Stuck on the plateau.* Sydney, Australia: JBWere.

Nelson, G., Westhues, A., Laurier, W., & MacLeod, J. (2003). A meta-analysis of longitudinal research on preschool prevention programs for children. *Prevention and Treatment, 6*, 1–35.

Olds, D. (2002). Prenatal and infancy home visiting by nurses: From randomized trials to community replication. *Prevention Science, 3*(3), 153–172.

Olds, D. (2012). *Nurse-family partnership: Blueprints program rating model.* Retrieved from http://www.blueprintsprograms.com/evaluation-abstract/nurse-family-partnership.

Olds, D., Kitzman, H., Cole, R., Robinson, J., Sidora, K., Luckey, D., . . . Holmberg, J. (2004). Effects of nurse home-visiting on maternal life course and child development: Age 6 follow-up results of a randomized trial. *Pediatrics, 114*(6), 1550–1559.

Olds, D., Robinson, J., Pettitt, L., Luckey, D., Holmberg, J., Ng, R., . . . Henderson, C. (2004). Effects of home visits by paraprofessionals and by nurses: Age 4 follow-up results of a randomized trial. *Pediatrics, 114*(6), 1560–1568.

Philanthropy Australia. (2013). *Annual report.* Melbourne, Australia.

Philanthropy Australia. (2014). *Fast facts and stats.* Retrieved from http://www.philanthropy.org.au/tools-resources/fast-facts-and-stats/.

Ramey, C., & Campbell, F. (1991). Poverty, early childhood education, and academic competence: The Abecedarian experiment. In A. Huston (Ed.), *Children in poverty: Child development and public policy* (pp. 190–221). Cambridge: Cambridge University Press.

Responsible Investment Association Australasia. (2014). *Responsible investment benchmark report: Australia and New Zealand.* Sydney, Australia.

Reynolds, A., Ou, S., & Topitzes, J. (2004). Paths of effects of early childhood intervention on educational attainment and delinquency: A confirmatory analysis of the Chicago child-parent centers. *Child Development, 75*(5), 1299–1328. doi:10.1111/j.1467–8624.2004.00742.x.

Reynolds, A., Temple, J., Ou, S., Arteaga, I., & White, B. (2011). School-based early childhood education and age-28 well-being: Effects by timing, dosage, and subgroups. *Science, 333*(6040), 360–364.

Reynolds, A., Temple, J., Ou, S., Robertson, D., Mersky, J., Topitzes, J., & Niles, M. (2007). Effects of a school-based, early childhood intervention on adult health and well-being: A 19-year follow-up of low-income families. *Archives of Pediatrics & Adolescent Medicine, 161*(8), 730–739.

Reynolds, A., Temple, J., Robertson, D., & Mann, E. (2002). Age 21 cost-benefit analysis of the title I Chicago child-parent centers. *Educational Evaluation and Policy Analysis, 24*, 267–303.

Rolnick, A., & Grunewald, R. (2003). Early childhood development: Economic development with a high public return. *The Region, 17*(4), 6–12.

Sanders, M. (2003). Triple P – Positive parenting program: A population approach to promoting competent parenting. *Australian e-Journal for the Advancement of Mental Health, 2*(3), 1–17.

Sanders, M., Markie-Dadds, C., & Turner, K. (2003). *Theoretical, scientific and clinical foundations of the Triple P – Positive parenting program: A population approach to the promotion of parenting competence.* Parenting Research and Practice Monograph No. 1, The Parenting and Family Support Centre.

Saper, C., Chou, T., & Elmquist, J. (2002). The need to feed: Homeostatic and hedonic control of eating. *Neuron, 36*(2), 199–211.

Schultz, T. (1963). *The economic value of education* (Vol. 63). New York: Columbia University Press.

Schultz, T. (1982). *Investing in people: The economics of population quality.* Los Angeles, CA: University of California Press.

Schweinhart, L.J., Montie, J., Xiang, Z., Barnett, W.S., Belfield, C.R., & Nores, M. (2005). *Lifetime effects: The HighScope Perry Preschool study through age 40.* Ypsilanti, Michigan: High/Scope Press.

Sparling, J., & Lewis, I. (1979). *Learningames for the first three years: A guide to parent-child play.* New York: Berkley Books.

Swanson, A., & King, R. (1991). *School finance: Its economics and politics.* New York: Longman Publishing Group.

Sweetland, S. (1996). Human capital theory: Foundations of a field of inquiry. *Review of Educational Research, 66*(3), 341–359.

Temple, J., & Reynolds, A. (2007). Benefits and costs of investments in preschool education: Evidence from the child–parent centers and related programs. *Economics of Education Review, 26*(1), 126–144.

Tremblay, R.E., Masse, B., Perron, D., LeBlanc, M., Schwartzman, A., & Ledingham, J. (1992). Early disruptive behavior, poor school achievement, delinquent behavior, and delinquent personality: Longitudinal analyses. *Journal of Consulting and Clinical Psychology, 60*(1), 64.

Vaizey, J. (1962). *The economics of education.* London: Faber and Faber.

Zeanah, C., & Zeanah, P. (2009). The scope of infant mental health. *Handbook of Infant Mental Health, 3*(1), 5–21.

Chapter 5

Developmental lifecourse theory perspectives in Australia

The fundamental aim of the developmental lifecourse perspective, or DLC, is to describe and explain changes over time in rates of deviance and delinquency at the individual level. DLC, however, does not address historical changes in rates. Rather, it examines the way deviance and delinquency develops over the lifecourse of the individual. Importantly, DLC is not limited to describing and explaining deviance and delinquency, but includes other developmental outcomes such as antisocial behaviour, disengagement in learning, bullying, poor educational outcomes and poor health to name a few. Early theoretical models have had significant influence on the research (mostly school-aged children and adolescents) conducted into antisocial behavior and poor educational outcomes; according to these early perspectives, children learn from their environment – for example from peers in the school playground. The onset of various behaviours is then triggered by an accumulated exposure to these models of behaviour, including what kids watch on television and the media. Recent longitudinal research, however, suggests an inverse developmental process. That is, children learn socially acceptable behaviour from interactions with their environment.

The purpose of this chapter is to examine the DLC evidence on early educational and social experiences, showing how early childhood educators have and can create a positive learning environment where children learn prosocial behaviours and skills to prepare them for the important transitions (e.g. preschool to primary school) in their life. This chapter also introduces educators, academics, students and practitioners to the important barriers to our knowledge and how these can be overcome using the traditional scientific method.

We begin this chapter by briefly introducing the DLC approach, making a clear distinction between developmental prevention and early intervention. In Section 2, principles of prevention are discussed including risk and protective factors and functional capabilities. We then elaborate on the contexts of prevention and the reasons for intervening early in the developmental pathway (Section 3). Section 4 briefly reviews the effectiveness of developmental prevention. Finally, Section 5 discusses the limitations with respect to our knowledge and how we overcome these to build better evidence around DLC.

88 Developmental lifecourse theory perspectives in Australia

It should be noted that we focus specifically on the benefits that arise from interventions implemented in the early years (e.g. preschool) on outcomes *post hoc* intervention to later in life (adolescence – e.g. later primary to secondary school years). The outcomes discussed in Section 4 mainly relate to non-health outcomes such as cognitive development, educational success, social-emotional development, deviance, social participation and family wellbeing. The focus is specifically on these outcomes, and not directly health- or crime-related, as longitudinal research on DLC strategies, namely preschool interventions (as the focus of this chapter), was typically developed with these at the forefront of their agenda.

The DLC perspective

Children who are disadvantaged due to social, economic and environmental factors, are unprepared for the transition to formal schooling (i.e. primary school), or display early signs of early disruptive behaviour are at a greater risk of developing social, health and psychological problems later in life (Homel, Elias, & Hay, 2001; Manning, 2008). Such 'deficiencies' or 'situations' have the potential to amplify over time and may result in undesirable trajectories that steer an individual down a path that hinders their potential to succeed or affect their quality of life and that of their future children. Poor outcomes that result from these deficiencies or situations could include, for example, poor educational outcomes (e.g. school drop-out, poor educational achievement), reduced economic success (e.g. welfare dependence), increased deviance and contact with the criminal justice system, poor employment prospects, family dysfunction and chronic health disease (Manning, Homel, & Smith, 2010).

The DLC perspective highlights a range of factors (e.g. individual, cultural, social, environmental and economic) that may affect, or have an influence upon, vulnerability. To fully understand vulnerability, and make the necessary changes to 'protect' or assist the individual to overcome adversity, one must consider the multiple causal factors that act upon individuals at the various stages across their life (e.g. birth, transition from home to formal schooling), acknowledging that different factors may be more or less important at varying stages across the life course. Homel (2005) states:

> Life . . . is not marked by one steady march towards adulthood whose direction becomes fixed after early childhood . . . instead, what occurs is a series of phases, a series of points of change, a series of transitions. These points of transition are when intervention can often occur most effectively, since at times of change individuals are both vulnerable to taking false steps and open to external support or advice
>
> (p. 81).

According to Homel these transition points can either serve to initiate or reinforce vulnerability or, if protective steps are taken, reduce vulnerability. In reality, almost all non-biological transitions require an individual to identify with new social institutions, many of these requiring an individual to cope with a new set of developmental tasks and challenges (Laub & Sampson, 2005). For example, some children are vulnerable when moving from home to a formal school setting (e.g. kindergarten, primary school). The transition into this new setting can be stressful, frightening and overwhelming if strategies are not put in place to protect the child and equip them with the necessary skills and resources to cope. These strategies are often needed before the transition (e.g. preparing to learn in the kindergarten years) or at the time of the transition (e.g. strategies aimed at reducing stress and uncertainty; this could be as simple as having an older 'buddy' to assist the child in negotiating a new and unfamiliar environment).

The difference between developmental prevention and early intervention

Subtle differences exist between the terms developmental prevention and early intervention. We highlight these below in an attempt to illuminate what is often a particularly dark and poorly understood area.

Developmental prevention

Four principles underpin developmental prevention: (1) 'developmental intervention' does not necessarily mean early in life, but 'early in the developmental pathway';[1] (2) context is always changing – this includes, but is not limited to, social policies, institutions and neighbourhoods; (3) risk and protective factors matter; and (4) interventions are most effective when the focus is placed on important transitions in an individual's life (Manning, 2008).

Developmental prevention involves planning and employing efforts to reduce undesirable trajectories, while preserving or increasing positive pathways for individuals, particularly those who are disadvantaged or vulnerable due to circumstances often beyond their control. Such prevention involves targeting risk and protective factors in order to alter potential negative pathways or trajectories with an emphasis on investing in institutions (e.g. schools or other learning environments such as playgroups), communities and social policies that manipulate multiple risk and protective factors at different levels of the social ecology, and at crucial transition points (e.g. the commencement of school, or graduation from primary to high school). In short, developmental prevention is about providing resources to overcome adversity at critical points in the individual's life, not only in the early years (Homel et al., 2006; Little, 1999).

Developmental pathways are distinguished from the more causal pathways models proposed by Hertzman (1999). Causal pathways are written from a medical or epidemiological perspective where there is an emphasis on " . . . linear causal chains of events" (Homel, 2005, p. 83). For example, one condition (e.g. poor school readiness) leads to another (e.g. disability and absenteeism in the fifth decade of life) via intermediate events (e.g. poor educational outcomes, working in a highly stressed, low control job) (Homel et al., 2006). Homel (2005) states:

> According to this model, much of the social gradient effect in health outcomes arises from the amplification and reproduction by social processes of the effects of differences in individual traits and in life circumstances at (or before) birth
> (p. 83).

Hertzman's hypothesis that certain conditions in the early years of life, particularly around emotional support and cognitive stimulation, *sculpt* neural and cognitive pathways permanently are not as radical as one may think. According to Keating and Hertzman (1999) neural sculpting is the process " . . . whereby the social and physical environments of an infant and young child organize the experiences that shape the networks and patterns of the brain" (p. 3). In the context of children who experience early disadvantage Hertzman (1999) states:

> Spending one's early years in an unstimulating, emotionally and physically unsupportive environment will affect the sculpting and neurochemistry of the central nervous system in adverse ways, leading to cognitive and socioemotional delays. The problems that children so affected will display early in school will lead them to experience much more acute and chronic stress than others, which will have both psychological and life path consequences . . . The process whereby human experience affects the healthfulness of life across the life cycle, is herein called biological embedding
> (p. 31).

The process whereby early experiences or vulnerabilities affect later life events or outcomes is known as biological embedding. In short, early experiences alter human biology and development. Researchers are now attempting to investigate this concept and question: how do early childhood environments work together, with genetic variation and epigenetic regulation, to generate gradients in health and human development across the life course?

In summary, the developmental pathways model and the causal pathways model are similar in many respects. They do, however, differ regarding one issue; the developmental pathways model acknowledges that human agency and the possibility of changing one's ways is achievable because of changes in social circumstances and opportunities that arise during an individual's lifecourse (Elder, 1998; Homel, 2005).

Early intervention

So what sets early intervention apart from developmental prevention? Early intervention begins by identifying individuals early in life as opposed to early in a developmental pathway. Early intervention begins by identifying those who are vulnerable. This could include, for example, low-income, first-time parents. Early interventions of this nature assist first-time parents to begin their lives with their children on a positive footing or trajectory in order to circumvent potential problems that may manifest into future health and antisocial behavioral problems. The intervention provides resources to assist the individual to mediate vulnerability through risk minimisation and protective enhancement strategies. Enhancing protective factors, with the goal of enriching the available pathways for an individual, typically involves the provision of access to experiences and services that compensate for adverse life circumstances, disadvantage and vulnerability (Hayes, 2006).

For example, prenatal and early childhood nurse home visitation programs underpinned by theory and validated by a series of randomized clinical trials, designed to develop and test the program model (Olds, 1988; Olds et al., 1997; Olds & Korfmacher, 1997), were established to:

- Assist pregnant women in improving their health – Doing this makes it more likely that their children will be born free of neurological problems.
- Teach first-time mothers how to care for their children and to provide a positive home environment – Doing this helps to ensure that children are nurtured, live in a safe environment within and around the home, are disciplined safely and consistently, and receive proper health care.
- Teach young parents to keep their lives on track by practicing birth control and planning future pregnancies – This assists parents in reaching their educational goals and finding adequate employment, which, in turn, assists the child in their development.

This form of intervention, as well as developmental intervention programs, can be delivered universally (i.e. efforts are placed on the whole population), targeted (i.e. population subgroups identified as at-risk) or indicated (i.e. individuals identified with a given problem, or at increased risk of its future development) (Gordon, 1983).

Figure 5.1 presents factors that have the potential to increase risk early in a child's life and lead to problems later in life (e.g. school failure, school drop-out, delinquency and contact with the criminal justice system). Arguably, by simultaneously preventing the accumulation of risk factors, which include health, social and environmental, through evidence-based and well-delivered comprehensive programs, families can get off to a strong start. This enables their children to develop and mature, devoid of health and developmental baggage.

The above figure explicitly reveals a pattern of deterioration. Revealing a series of factors (which are symbiotic in nature) that have both internal and external loci (e.g. political and macroeconomic systems),[2] adversity is clearly multiplied when the individual does not successfully negotiate key phases in their life. For example, subtle damage to the developing fetal nervous system due to Fetal Alcohol

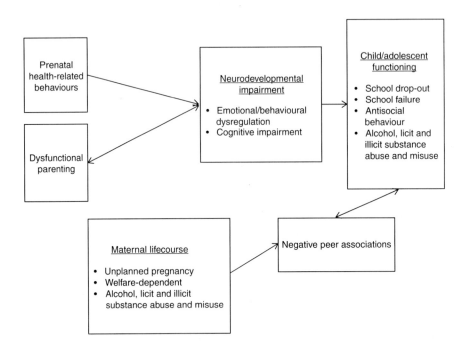

Figure 5.1 Model of Program Influences on Conduct Disorder and Antisocial Behaviour

Adapted from Olds et al. (1999)

Spectrum Disorder (FASD), caused by exposure to alcohol during pregnancy (Sokol, Delaney-Black, & Nordstrom, 2003), can culminate into a spectrum of disorders including:

- Fetal alcohol syndrome (FAS), where a child has problems with growth and learning, and has distinctive facial features and structural abnormalities due to alcohol exposure during pregnancy;
- Partial FAS, where a child has some, but not all, features reported in FAS;
- Alcohol-related neuro-developmental disorders (ARND), where a child has problems with learning and behaviour related to alcohol exposure; and
- Alcohol-related birth defects (ARBD), where abnormalities in a child's organs such as the heart or kidneys occur due to fetal alcohol exposure.

Following Figure 5.1, and using ARND as an example, the disorder interferes with child's capacity to respond effectively to their parents' efforts to care for them, including in their social, emotional and educational development (O'Malley, 2015). Such interference can establish patterns of frustration and anger, which have the potential of influencing, negatively, child-parent attachment (Caspi et al., 1995; Moffitt, 1993b; Rodning, Beckwith, & Howard, 1989; Sanson et al., 1993). This is compounded by inconsistent and sometimes harsh discipline as the parent/s themselves become impatient and irritable (Bodenmann, Cina, Ledermann, & Sanders, 2008; Huh et al., 2006). This can be, in part, explained by genetic links, overwhelming stress and substance abuse (Olds, Hill, & Ramsey, 1998). A vicious cycle is created whereby the child's problems with emotional and behavioral regulation further contribute to, and sometimes intensify, parental abuse and neglect, which further creates more imbalance in the child's emotional and behavioral regulation (Olds et al., 1986). This type of scenario is more frequent in large families (Hirschi & Gottfredson, 1994) who are financially stressed (Conger et al., 1993). Unfortunately, it may well be the case that children who are further exposed to these environments [low socio-economic] may be further affected or influenced, particularly during adolescence, by deviant peers (Felner et al., 1995; Hirschi, 1994; Moffitt, 1993a). In addition, children who are part of this disadvantaged group (e.g. low income, family dysfunction due to inconsistent and harsh parenting, parents with poor educational background) tend to be corralled into educational support programs (e.g. language support), where their placement tends to intensify or worsen their behavioral and academic problems. This is often due to peer influence as these groups tend to be made up of other children with similar problems. To complicate the issue, children who are removed from their regular classroom are often disadvantaged again as it interferes with their socialisation process. Doing this makes reintegration complicated and often difficult to achieve successfully (GHK Consulting – Holden McAllister Partnership and IPSOS Public Affairs, 2004; Manning, 2004). Finally, vulnerable children tend to be more susceptible to rejection by prosocial peers and to negative peer influences (Coie et al., 1995; Dishion et al., 1995). It is nearly always the case that the school confronts the parents of children who display social, educational and sometimes developmental deficiencies. In some cases, this may further harm the child as they may further reject the child or discipline them excessively, which potentially pushes the children further toward delinquency and crime (Coie, 1996).

Principles of DLC

Risk and protective factors

Risk and protective factors underpin the DLC perspective. So what is a risk factor? Risk factors are measurable characteristics that precede an outcome and are used to divide the population of interest into a range of risk groups (e.g. high and low risk). They can be classified as fixed (e.g. race and gender) or variable (e.g. parental child rearing practices and levels of social and educational support).

What is a protective factor? These are variables that reduce the probability of negative outcomes – for example, the presence of a stable emotional bond to a

94 Developmental lifecourse theory perspectives in Australia

caregiver. What is important to note is that little is achieved by calling the low-risk end of a risk dimension a protective factor (Rutter, 2000). For example, if having parents who do not provide a nurturing (including assisting in learning by reading to the child) and emotionally supportive environment is a risk factor, the absence of a poor emotional family environment is not necessarily going to protect you against other risk factors that might be encountered throughout life. Rather, we should conceptualise a protective factor to be more than just the absence of a risk factor.

It is also important to understand that what may be a risk factor in one situation may be a protective factor in another. Risk and protective factors, in some situations, potentially function simultaneously. For example, the divorce of a child's parents might have a negative impact on some children and may constitute a risk factor. Conversely, a volatile family environment coupled with marital conflict and perhaps even domestic violence is likely to have a negative impact on the child's social and emotional wellbeing, so divorce may actually act as a protective device from children being subjected to further stress. Das (2010) found this to be the case in minority ethnic families whose culture is highly resistant to divorce.

Functional capabilities

Developmental prevention proposes that not all children are born healthy, provided with adequate health care, have access to good nutrition, or live in acceptable housing conditions; not all children are born free of disabilities, or are raised by parents who can comfort, nurture and provide adequate language, literacy, social problem-solving and behaviour management skills. Therefore, as discussed above, the DLC perspective aims to augment a child's development by providing access to experiences and services that support the child and their family to assist in shaping later life experiences (Rutter, 2007). Starting early in life is important. At this stage in the lifecourse individuals can minimise the effect of adverse life circumstances, disadvantage and vulnerability, and shape opportunities for developing new pathways that ultimately promote improved quality of life (Meisels & Shonkoff, 2000).

Quality of life may be defined as subjective wellbeing, the latter reflecting the difference between the expectations and hopes of a person and their present experiences; in other words, the degree to which a person enjoys the important possibilities of their life. Possibilities are a consequence of opportunities and limitations each person has in their life and reflect the interaction of personal, social, environmental and economic factors (Diener, Suh, & Oishi, 1997). One should note that it is not only real opportunities and limitations that limit possibilities, but perceived opportunities and limitations as well.

A conceptual framework developed by Sen and Nussbaum (1996) emphasise the role of functional capabilities of individuals. Sen and Nussbaum stress the importance of acknowledging the functional capabilities (e.g. individual freedoms including the ability to live to an old age, engage in economic transactions and participate in political activities) of individuals as well as individual utility (e.g. happiness) and access to resources (e.g. income and assets) when evaluating social states in terms of wellbeing. Here, poverty would be classified as a capability-deprivation. Sen and Nussbaum suggest that emphasis should not be placed on how humans actually function, but their capability to function. Capability-deprivation could come about as a result of ignorance, government oppression, lack of financial resources or false consciousness. Sen and Nussbaum, therefore, emphasise the importance of freedom of choice and the acknowledgement of individual heterogeneity (i.e. individual differences) when considering the wellbeing of individuals. This has important implications for educators, as modern pedagogy emphasises the significance of acknowledging the individual and their unique strengths, as well as their ability to have input into their learning across the lifecourse (Homel et al., 2006).

The context of prevention

The 20th century saw a general improvement in quality of life of people as well as a dramatic decline in rates of mortality (The World Health Organisation, 1999). For example, life expectancy in England and Wales in the 200 years prior to the 1870s varied around an average of 40 years. The subsequent (i.e. from 1870s to 1990s) 125 years saw life expectancy almost double as demonstrated in Table 5.1.

In Australia in the 20th-century age-standardized death rates have been falling (Figure 5.2) where rates fell by 64 per cent for males (from 2,370 deaths per 100,000 population in 1900 to 853 in 2000) and 72 per cent for females (from 1,957 deaths per 100,000 population to 552 in 2000) (Australian Institute of Health and Welfare, 2005).

The life expectancy of young people has increased significantly over the 20th century (Figure 5.3). In 2000, a male aged one could expect to live to the age of 78 years and females to 83, while in the 1900s the life expectancy of males and

Table 5.1 Life Expectancy at Birth around 1910 and in 1998

Country	Around 1910		In 1998	
	Males	*Females*	*Males*	*Females*
Australia	56	60	75	81
New Zealand	60	63	74	80
Japan	43	43	77	83
England and Wales	49	53	75	80
Italy	46	47	75	81
Sweden	57	59	76	81
Norway	56	59	75	81
United States	49	53	73	80

Adapted from: The World Health Organisation (1999)

96 Developmental lifecourse theory perspectives in Australia

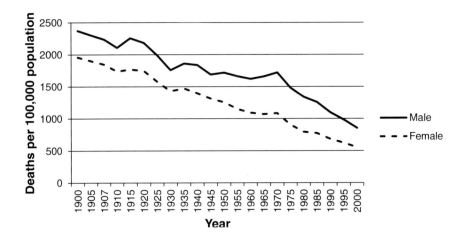

Figure 5.2 Trends in Rates of Mortality (All-Cause) from 1900 to 2000

females aged one year was 66 and 69, respectively (Australian Institute of Health and Welfare, 2005).

Similarly, life expectancy has increased markedly with males aged 30 years of age expected to live to the age of 78 years and females 83 years (based on 2000–2002 figures) compared to the 1900s where males aged 30 were expected to live to 66 years of age and females 69 years (Figure 5.4). This equates to approximately a 20 per cent increase in life expectancy at age 30 over the 20th century (Australian Institute of Health and Welfare, 2005).

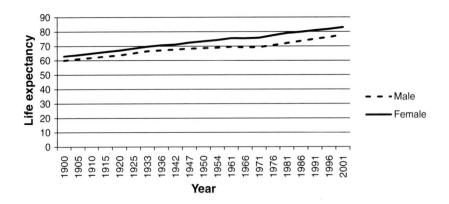

Figure 5.3 Trends in Life Expectancy for Males and Females Aged One Year (1900–2000)

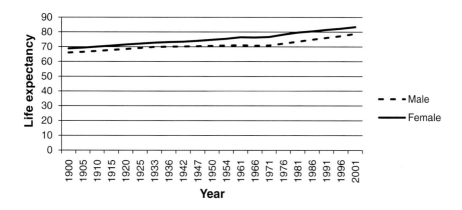

Figure 5.4 Trends in Life Expectancy for Males and Females Aged 30 Years (1900–2000)

The final system, the *macrosystem*, contains all of the various subsystems and the various beliefs and values that are embedded within a culture via unwritten principles that regulate individual and collective behavior. These principles, for example, may be legal, economic, political, religious or educational. The principles endow an individual's life with meaning and value. In addition, the principles control the nature and scope of interactions between the various systems. Later, Bronfenbrenner added an additional system, the *chronosystem*. This system comprises all other systems and refers to the bi-directional influence of each system and the importance of history regarding a child's development. For example, times of economic depression, war, or technological development can either positively or negatively influence a child's development (Bronfenbrenner & Morris, 2006).

According to Bronfenbrenner, families who live and work in stressed and disorganised environments find it difficult to provide the necessary conditions that nurture the important dimensions of children's development, including learning and social and emotional development. For example, Freiberg et al. (2010) state:

> When families are alienated by hardship and overwhelmed by the strain of conditions – such as poverty, work pressures, relationship problems, mental illness, domestic violence, or substance abuse – they may not have the skill, will, support or access to the kind of external resources that enable them to provide for their children's basic physical and emotional needs or to keep them safe from harm, let alone to provide the kind of experiences that will foster the physical, cognitive, linguistic, social and emotional skills their children need in order to succeed in relationships with others, at school and in adult life . . . Schools are often unprepared for the challenge of supporting the learning of children . . . who arrive at school with under- or

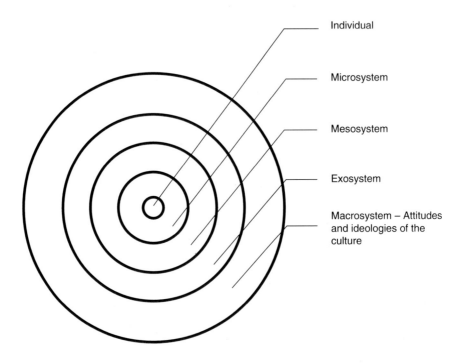

Figure 5.5 Bronfenbrenner's Ecological Framework for Human Development

Income growth, improved access to education (which, in turn, led to improved levels of education), improvements in food intake and sanitation account for some of the decline in rates of mortality and increases in life expectancy. Also important was the development of a system of research centers (resulting in access to new knowledge, drugs and vaccines), hospitals, clinics and specialised diagnostic and emergency departments (The World Health Organisation, 1999). The 20th century also produced a number of significant developments in areas such as power (e.g. the building of new power plants, the use of fossil fuels, hydro and nuclear power and nationwide systems of distribution facilities thus improving efficiency, increasing reliability and reducing costs), motor transport (e.g. mass production of automobiles and trucks and building of highway systems), telecommunications (e.g. creating systems ranging from telephone and radio to television and satellite communications) and food (e.g. the provision of an abundant and stable supply of food via improved agriculture, new processing plants, refrigeration and innovations in packaging and distribution).

Bronfenbrenner (2005) notes, however, that although these changes (e.g. access to education, food intake, sanitation) have enhanced quality of life by providing safer and better jobs, building a strong and resilient economic base and supporting social structures that improve the everyday lives of people, these changes have begun to threaten the social and ethical development of children. This is particularly the case for those who grow up outside the mainstream communities that have been somewhat marginalised by changes in the social, economic and environmental fabric of modern society. As such, the functional capabilities of these children are somewhat limited. Alongside the general improvements we have witnessed in mainstream communities, lie growing rates of disruptive behaviour, delinquency, depression, suicide, substance use, lack of connection and poor school performance of the more marginalised communities (Stanley, Richardson, & Prior, 2005).

Ecological theory (Bronfenbrenner, 1979) and developmental systems theory (e.g. Lerner, 2012; Lerner & Overton, 2008) are used to examine child development, and to explain the adverse trajectories in the developmental outcomes of vulnerable children. According to these theories, social change partly explains a range of modern conditions (e.g. stress, family breakdown and dysfunction, poverty and inadequate parental engagement) that have begun to interfere with "proximal processes" (Freiberg, Homel, & Branch, 2010) that are important to positive development and also functional capabilities. These proximal processes include nurturing and responsive parenting and strong supportive relationships within the family environment and between the family and institutions in which children live and operate (e.g. home, school, neighbourhood and community) (Freiberg et al., 2010).

Bronfenbrenner (1979) identified four systems that contain rules, norms and roles that help to shape human development (Figure 5.5). The goal of this systems approach was to answer the key question: how does the world around the child help or hinder their development? Bronfenbrenner noted that development is the result of the relationships that occur between a person and their environment. Importantly, one cannot evaluate development only in the immediate environment; one must also examine the interactions that occur among the larger environments in which an individual develops.

The *microsystem*, the first of four systems, defines the immediate environment, the layer in which the child has the most direct contact. These include, for example, the family, school, peer group, neighbourhood and other institutions of care such as childcare and early learning centers. Bronfenbrenner highlighted that this layer is bifacial with respect to impact away and toward the child. For example, a child's parents may affect their beliefs (e.g. value of education) and behaviour; however, the child also affects the behaviour and beliefs of the parent. The second system, the *mesosystem*, comprises of connections between the child's immediate environments. For example, if a child experiences difficulties at school, it is likely that the child's parent/s will need to interact with teachers and administrators at the school. This interaction will no doubt have an effect on the child's functioning within both environments. The *exosystem*, the third system, contains other external and social systems that affect a child's development (e.g. the parent's workplace, neighbourhood institutions, the media, the government and the local economy).

100 Developmental lifecourse theory perspectives in Australia

inappropriately developed skills and are largely unprepared for the challenges of the education system . . . [having] undeveloped communication skills; lack competence in peaceful interpersonal problem-solving but are skilled in the use of manipulative and aggressive survival techniques, with little apparent regard for the feelings of others; and are distrustful or suspicious of authority figures. Such challenges to teaching and classroom management can create the feeling of being besieged . . . This often sets up an adversarial situation that may include blaming families for student failure. This is nearly always counterproductive because it erodes links between the critical developmental contexts of home and school

(p. 29).

The important message being made by Freiberg and her colleagues is that when schools become distracted or overwhelmed by the " . . . by-products of 'toxic' developmental settings" (p. 30) they tend to expend resources and energy and are often " . . . locked in a continuing cycle of reaction to developmental difficulties" (p. 30). As a consequence, teachers become exhausted by stress " . . . to work proactively to create conditions that support children's learning and promote developmental competence" (p. 30). Distracted teachers increase the likelihood that vulnerable children further fall behind and, in turn, jeopardise long-term prospects and future quality of life (Knudson et al., 2006).

This raises an important question: how do we provide children the opportunity to succeed – particularly those who are considered vulnerable in our society? According to developmental systems theory, prevention should be holistic in nature and draw upon the strengths of individuals and their communities. In Lerner's words, "the role of developmental science is to identify those relations between individual strengths and contextual assets in families, communities, cultures, and the natural environment, and to integrate strengths and assets to promote positive human development" (2006, p. 12). The next question is when do we begin intervention efforts and for how long?

Why do we begin interventions early?

The consensus among the scientific community is that we begin as early as we can. The temporal boundaries of prevention have been described by some as 'womb to tomb'. This means that we begin providing resources antenatal and continue to provide resources and opportunities, at key life transitions or times of need, over the entire lifecourse. However, this does not mean that the early years are the only ones that matter. All is not lost if we do not 'treat' or 'provide' in the early years of a child's life. We should do everything in our power to identify those who are at risk or are vulnerable however, and provide access to early health and developmental resources where necessary. To be clear, early childhood should not be considered a critical period where irreversible harm is done to the individual in the absence of early prevention (Bruer, 1999). Rather, early childhood should be considered as the first point in a series of important life phases, each of which contain aspects of vulnerability and opportunity (Laub & Sampson, 2005). Rather than suggesting that once past the age of three there is no possibility of brain development and restructuring, we should consider this point as a critical time for learning as suggested by Hockfield and Lombroso (1998). For example, many cognitive and motor skills are gained quickly during the early years of life, but after this period such skills are not mastered as easily. To demonstrate this theory, Hockfiled and Lombroso used acquisition of a second language. If a child learns a second language early, both the native and second language are represented in the same cortical region. In contrast, when a second language is acquired in adulthood, a new language centre that is clearly separated from the native language centre is established in the cortex (Hockfield & Lombroso, 1998, p. 2). Hockfield and Lombroso imply that although this does not explain why children are able to learn a language more easily than an adult, it does suggest that early experiences do have an effect on brain development.

The point is it is never too late to learn or change given the plasticity of humans, particularly young humans. But the process becomes increasingly complex and difficult. Although the brain reaches its full size in adolescence, it " . . . continues to be malleable throughout an individual's lifetime, although the regions of the brain where synaptic restructuring occurs vary by age" (Solso cited in Karoly et al., 1998, p. 3). McCain et al. (1999) reveal similar findings, but they are more skeptical about the possibility of brain development at an older age. They state: "once the critical periods for brain development are passed, providing the child has not experienced extreme neglect, it is possible to develop the brain's capacity to compensate but it is difficult to achieve its full potential" (p. 6).

The evidence

Heckman (2015) proposes four big benefits of investing in DLC prevention. Specifically, he states early intervention:

- Can prevent the achievement gap – Gaps in knowledge and ability between disadvantaged children and their more advantaged peers open up long before kindergarten, tend to persist throughout life, and are difficult and costly to close. Taking a proactive approach to cognitive and social skill development through investments in quality early childhood programs is more effective and economically efficient than trying to close the gap later on.
- Can improve health outcomes – More than 30 years later, treatment group individuals were at significantly lower risk for serious cardiovascular and metabolic diseases, such as stroke and diabetes. These findings demonstrate the great potential of coordinated birth-to-age-five early childhood programs to prevent chronic disease, reduce health care costs and produce a flourishing society.
- Can boost earnings – Extremely disadvantaged children in Jamaica who took part in an early intervention similar to home visiting programs in the United

States boosted their earnings in adulthood by 25 per cent, putting their wages on par with those of their more advantaged peers (Heckman, 2015, p. 1).

- Makes economic sense – The rate of return for investments in quality early childhood development for disadvantaged children is 7–10 per cent per annum through better outcomes in education, health, sociability, economic productivity and reduced crime (p. 1).

Empirical evidence suggests that early childhood intervention programs that employ a risk-focused approach (targeting those who are considered at risk at an early age) appear to be producing positive results, particularly in the short term (Manning, 2008). These studies have confirmed improved outcomes for those targeted across multiple domains including improved educational outcomes, decreases in child maltreatment, reductions in child and youth antisocial behaviour, lower levels of substance abuse, and increases in income and workforce participation (Brooks-Gunn, Fuligni, & Berlin, 2003; Olds, 2002; Reynolds et al., 2001). McCain et al. (1999) argue that efficacious developmental programs, that involve parents or other primary caregivers, can influence how caregivers relate to and care for the children, and can vastly improve a child's outcomes for behaviour, learning and health in later life. Moreover, the authors suggest that the benefits extend to all socio-economic groups in society. Heckman, Stixrud, and Urzua (2006) stress the importance of the family in mediating the cognitive and social-emotional skills of children in their early years. Their research highlights that families who *do* invest in developing their child's cognitive and social-emotional skills (non-cognitive) significantly improve their child's life trajectory – with reductions in subsequent involvement in crime, reduced probability of teenage pregnancy and improved educational outcomes.

A number of meta-analyses have been conducted highlighting the effectiveness of prevention models (e.g. family-based prevention, home-visitation, parenting programs, enriched preschool programs) on a range of outcomes (e.g. offending, cognitive development, educational attainment, social-emotional development, social participation, health and familial wellbeing) ranging from directly after the intervention to early adulthood (Farrington & Welsh, 2003; MacLeod & Nelson, 2000; Manning, 2008; Manning et al., 2010; Nelson et al., 2003).

Manning et al. (2010) conducted a meta-analytic review of early developmental prevention programs (children aged 0–5: structured preschool programs, centre-based developmental day care, home visitation, family support services and parental education) delivered to at-risk populations on non-health outcomes during adolescence (educational success, cognitive development, social-emotional development, deviance, social participation, involvement in criminal justice, and family wellbeing) (Table 5.2).

Their review improved on previous meta-analyses as it included a more comprehensive set of adolescent outcomes, focused on measures that are psychometrically valid, and it included a more detailed analysis of program moderator effects. Seventeen studies, based on 11 interventions (all U.S.-based) were included in the analysis (see Table 5.3).

Table 5.2 Outcome Domains and Operationalisations

Outcome domains	Operationalisations
Educational success (ES)	Special education; feeling of belonging at school; graduation; school drop-out; long-term school suspension; grade retention; completed years of education; school attendance (e.g. >20 absent days from school per year); learning problems
Cognitive development (CD)	IQ; achievement tests; school grades; rating of academic skill and performance; school failure.
Social-emotional development (SED)	Parent/teacher rating of problem behavior; social skills; self-esteem; self-confidence; obsessive-compulsive behavior
Deviance (D)	Rates of delinquent behavior; drug use (e.g. marijuana and alcohol); lying about age (e.g. false ID); running away from home; caught breaking the law; gang involvement
Social participation (SP)	Casual employment in teen years; socio-economic success; engaged in skilled jobs (e.g. electrician); makes active response to problems
Criminal justice (CJ)	Rates of juvenile arrest; rates of violent and non-violent arrest; incarceration; petition requests to juvenile court; adjudicated as a person in need of supervision due to incorrigible behavior (PINS)
Family wellbeing (FW)	Child maltreatment; parent-adolescent relationship; family functioning; parental mental health; parental employment/education; parental social support; quality of parenting; adolescent influence in family decisions; single-parent families; parental involvement in schooling; discrepancy between mother's occupational aspirations for child and child's own aspirations; child abuse and neglect; feeling of family unity

Source: Manning et al. (2010)

Table 5.3 Programs Included in the Manning et al. (2010) Study

Intervention Citation/Country of study	Study design (randomised design – yes/no)	Program length	Sample Size Intervention (En)	Sample Size Control (Cn)	Child's age at follow-up	Outcomes
Abecedarian Project (Campbell et al., 2002; Campbell & Ramey, 1994, 1995) United States of America	EE group (8 years of intervention – 5 years kindergarten + 3 years primary school) and EC group (5 years intervention – preschool only) (yes)	8 years (EE group) 5 years (EC group)	En = 53	Cn = 51	Age 12, 15 and 20	Academic achievement, cognitive, adult cognitive outcomes, adult reading grade equivalent, adult math grade equivalent, school success (post-secondary academic), completed school years, high school graduation, adult employment, socio-economic success (self-supporting), teen pregnancy reduction, social responsibility (misdemeanour, felony, incarceration, drug use)
Parent-Child Development Centres (PCDs) (Johnson, 2006; Johnson & Blumenthal, 2004) United States of America	Matched control (no)	5 Years	En = 84	Cn =160	Age 13–16	Academic achievement/school performance, mother and family development/family functioning, child behaviour problems

Chicago Child-Parent Centre (Reynolds, 1994; Reynolds et al., 2001) United States of America	CPC preschool vs. Comparison group (no)	2 years and 4–6 extended	En = 989	Cn = 550	Age 12, 16 and 20 years	Cognitive, social emotional, school success (special education, high school graduation, school drop out, grade retention), social responsibility (juvenile arrest, multiple arrests by 18 years, rates of violent and non-violent arrest)
Early Training Project (Gray & Klaus, 1970; Lazar & Darlington, 1982) United States of America	Home visitation and preschool vs. Control (yes)	2 and 3 years	En = 61	Cn = 27	End of Preschool age 9–10 years, 16 years	Child cognitive and language development, personal behaviour, social/emotional
Elmira Prenatal/ Early Infancy Project (Eckenrode et al., 2000; Olds et al., 1998) United States of America	Intervention vs. Control (yes)	3 years	En(*) = 184 En(**) = 38	Cn(*) = 116 Cn(**) = 62	Age 15 years	Social/emotional Criminal and antisocial behaviour
Learning to Learn (Sprigle & Schaefer, 1985) United States of America	Learning to Learn vs. Head Start (no)	3 years	En = 44	Cn = 39	Age 12	Cognitive, social-emotional outcomes

(Continued)

Table 5.3 (Continued)

Intervention Citation/Country of study	Study design (randomised design – yes/no)	Program length	Sample Size Intervention (En)	Sample Size Control (Cn)	Child's age at follow-up	Outcomes
Louisville Experiment (Miller & Bizzell, 1983) United States of America	Preschool interventions vs. Control (yes)	1 Year	En = 114	Cn =36	Age 13	Cognitive outcomes
Mother-Child Home Program (Levenstein et al., 1998) United States of America	Home-based intervention with mothers vs. Control (yes)	>1 year- 2 years	Full 2 year En = 70	Less than 2 year Cn = 38 No program n = 15	Age 13, 17 and 22 years	Social-emotional outcomes, cognitive, high school graduation, school drop-out
Perry Preschool Program (Berrueta-Clement et al., 1984) United States of America	Perry Preschool vs. Control (yes)	2 years	Preschool En = 68 Age 13 En = 68 Age 18 En = 55	Preschool Cn = 65 Age 13 Cn = 65 Age 18 Cn = 62	Preschool, age 13, 18	Social-emotional, personal behaviour, social development, academic skills, personal behaviour, school success, cognitive outcomes, effects on deviance and social patterns (e.g. delinquent

						behaviour, threatened or injured another person, employment, self-confidence), special education, high school graduation, school drop-out, post secondary academic and vocational training, social responsibility (e.g. juvenile arrest, multiple arrests by 18 years, adult arrests), effects on socio-economic success (e.g. employment/ unemployment, annual income, self-supporting), effects on health, family, and children in mid-life
The Syracuse Family Research Development Program (FDRP) (Lally, Mangione, & Honig, 1988) United States of America	Multi-component vs. comparison (no)	5 years	Preschool En = 82	Preschool Cn = 74	Preschool, 13–15 years of age	Cognitive, social-emotional, social responsibility (e.g. juvenile arrests, violent arrest)

(Continued)

Table 5.3 (Continued)

Intervention Citation/Country of study	Study design (randomised design – yes/no)	Program length	Sample Size Intervention (En)	Sample Size Control (Cn)	Child's age at follow-up	Outcomes
Direct Instruction project (Meyer, 1984) United States of America	DISTAR follow through vs. comparison (no)	3–4 years	En = 65	Cn = 100	18–20 years of age	Educational success (e.g. school graduation, retention, school drop-out, accepted for college). Cognitive development (e.g. ninth grade reading and math scores)

Source: Manning et al. (2010)

The mean effect size (Cohen's *d*) across all programs and outcomes was 0.313, equivalent to a 62 per cent higher mean score for an intervention group than for a control group. The largest effect was for educational success during adolescence (effect size *d*=0.53) followed by social deviance (*d*=0.48), social participation (*d*=0.37), cognitive development (*d*=0.34), involvement in criminal justice (*d*=0.24), family wellbeing (*d*=0.18), and social-emotional development (*d*=0.16) (Figure 5.6).

The authors also found that programs that lasted longer than three years were associated with larger sample means than programs that were longer than one year but shorter than three years. More intense programs (those with more than 500 sessions per participant) also had larger means than less intense programs. There was a marginally significant trend for programs with a follow-through component into the early primary school years (e.g. preschool to grade 3) to have more positive effects than programs without a follow-through.

Nelson et al. (2003) conducted a meta-analysis of longitudinal research on preschool prevention programs for children. Their goal was to determine the effectiveness of preschool prevention programs for disadvantaged children and their families in the short term (preschool years), the medium term (kindergarten to grade 8) and the long term (high school and beyond). Thirty-four preschool programs were included in the analysis. These programs had at least one follow-up assessment when the children were in their formal schooling years. Results reveal impacts were greatest on the children's cognitive development during the preschool period (*d*=0.52); these results persist through to grade 8, however, the effects dissipate over time (*d*=0.30). These results are similar to those found in previous studies (Hubbell et al., 1985; Lazar & Darlington, 1982) highlighting that immediate impacts on a child's cognitive development are much greater than

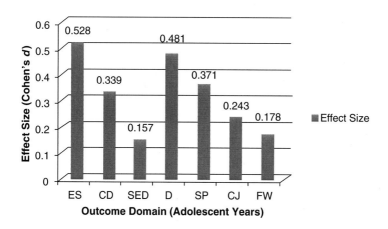

Figure 5.6 Weighted Average Effect Sizes (*d*) Corrected for Sample Size
Source: Manning et al. (2010)

110 Developmental lifecourse theory perspectives in Australia

medium-term impacts. Similarly, there were social-emotional impacts on children at grade 8 ($d=0.27$) and high school and beyond ($d=0.33$) and parent-family wellness impacts during preschool ($d=0.33$) and at grade 8 ($d=0.30$). As the researchers anticipated, cognitive gains during the preschool years were greatest for those programs that had a direct teaching component (i.e. with a preschool or centre-based educational component). This finding is consistent with previous reviews (Cohen & Radford, 1999; Ramey & Landesman Ramey, 1998). Further, those programs that had a follow-through component into elementary/primary school had better effects than those that did not. These findings are consistent with earlier narrative reviews (McLoyd, 1998; Ramey & Landesman Ramey, 1998). In short, a one-off inoculation in the preschool years is not enough to ensure long-term educational success. Supplements are important! The question that needs further research here is: how much more educational intervention is required before a plateau is reached in terms of a child's cognitive development? Greater results were also produced for those programs that were longer and more intensive. In short, both length and intensity of program are important moderators of some of the outcome indicators that were found to be heterogeneous. The average weighted effect sizes for those programs that were longer ($d=0.37$) and more intense ($d=0.44$) were much higher than those programs that were shorter in length ($d=0.11$) and less intensive ($d=0.18$) (Nelson et al., 2003). Interestingly, the authors did not find evidence to support the notion that programs that begin working with children at a younger age are more effective than those that begin when children are older. This finding is in contrast to the findings of Cohen and Radford (1999) and Ramey and Landesman Ramey (1998). Finally, the authors did not find evidence to support the hypothesis that multicomponent programs are more effective than programs that only have one or two components. Caution is warranted here as although there may be little difference in terms of effect size, multicomponent programs do offer a web of support for families that meet a variety of different needs including income support and access to other critical services (Febbraro, 1994). The effects may not be captured, as they are not having direct impacts on children outcomes (Manning, 2008).

Falsifiability

One should be cautious with the claims being made and the scientific rigour that underpins the study – in sum, the reliability and validity/generalizability of findings produced by many early childhood intervention studies. Many studies are no more than correlational in nature. There are studies although that can be considered scientifically rigorous. Those that are not, however, often lack some or most of the five necessary ingredients that we strive for in social science research: (1) regularity and generalizability – this refers to relations between concepts, which are stated as hypotheses or propositions; (2) reliability and replicability – this refers to explicating the steps by which the hypotheses are subject to empirical assessment; (3) validity – this relates to internal and external generalization; (4) prognostication or prediction – under *ceteris paribus* conditions, we should use conclusions from existing confirmed hypotheses and extend them to other unobserved phenomena; and (5) parsimony – this postulates that the number and complexity of causal hypotheses used should be limited and they should not be deducible from each other (Occam's razor – law of parsimony).

Falsifiability should be a necessary condition underpinning science, including the social sciences. Popper (1959) highlights that falsifiability defines the inherent testability of any scientific hypothesis. Falsifiability is the belief that for any hypothesis to have credence, it must be inherently disprovable before it can become accepted as a scientific hypothesis or theory. Popper saw falsifiability as a black and white definition, that if a theory is falsifiable, it is scientific, and if not, then it is unscientific. The advantage of Popper's idea is that such truths can be falsified when more knowledge and resources are available. Even long accepted theories can be, and should be, challenged and adapted.

DLC has produced a catalogue of potential explanations regarding the developmental trajectory of individuals. For example, why do some people easily negotiate life while others do not? What puts some individuals at risk of criminal involvement and not others? Why do some children fail at school while others succeed? Most of the explanations for human behavior draw on biological, cognitive, social, economic, situational, environmental and procedural domains. These explanations typically identify complex interactions of factors operating at individual, peer and societal levels, over immediate, short and long time scales, which in turn put individuals at risk or protect them from it.

If we focus on early delinquency, DLC theory proposes a wealth of factors that explain this 'condition'. These include, but are not limited to, high impulsivity and self-control (Farrington, 1994; White et al., 1994); intelligence (Lynam, Moffitt, & Stouthamer-Loeber, 1993); brain maturation (Steinberg, 2009); attention deficit disorder and early delinquency (Moffitt, 1990); behavioral risk and protective factors (Straus, Gelles, & Smith, 1990); substance-related disorders; schizophrenic and other psychotic disorders; mood disorders; sexual and gender identity disorders; personality disorders (Franklin, 2014); significant life events (Sampson & Laub, 1990); criminal families (Farrington, Coid, & Murray, 2009); neighborhood factors (Wikstrom & Loeber, 2000); attachment and socialization processes (Rankin & Kern, 1994); delinquent peers (Matsueda & Anderson, 1998); and childhood economic disadvantage (Fergusson, Swain-Campbell, & Horwood, 2004).

Such collections of proposed influences have become increasingly unwieldy. Their validity is extraordinarily difficult to test empirically. Furthermore, there are widely acknowledged weaknesses in the standard of evidence drawn on to identify them. Possible causes have therefore accrued without adequate testing or cumulative understanding – key requirements for the development of scientific knowledge. We suggest that explanations be parsimonious, sufficient, testable and falsifiable.

112 Developmental lifecourse theory perspectives in Australia

Final note

In summary, DLC has a great deal to offer policy makers, educators, academics, students and practitioners who are striving to improve the social, emotional, psychological, educational, economic and health outcomes of children, particularly those most vulnerable in our population and at risk of developing problems later in life. The evidence, although sparse and fragmented in terms of quality in some respects, is there supporting early intervention and subsequent intervention/s over critical periods of an individual's life, however, more must be done to improve the quality of the evidence base. Unless this is done, the veracity of the DLC approach will always be questioned and funding will always be limited and fragmented with governments and NGOs unwilling to invest, in the long term, in 'falsifiable-less' research. That is, research that lacks adequate testing or cumulative understanding of a problem or issue.

Notes

1   "A developmental pathway is defined as the orderly behavioral development between more than two problem behaviors with individuals differing in their propensity to progress along the successive problem behavior represented by the pathway during development. Thus, pathways are a window into dynamic rather than static individual differences in youths' progression to serious problem behaviors" (Loeber & Burke, 2011).
2   See discussion regarding the Bronfenbrenner and ecological and developmental systems theory later in the chapter.

References

Australian Institute of Health and Welfare. (2005). *Mortality over the twentieth in Australia: Trends and patterns in major causes of death.* Canberra, Australia.

Berrueta-Clement, J.R., Schweinhart, L.J., Barnett, S.W., Epstein, A.S., & Weikart, D.P. (1984). *Changes lives: The effects of the Perry Preschool Program on youths through age 19.* Ypsilanti, MI: High/Scope Educational Research Foundation.

Bodenmann, G., Cina, A., Ledermann, T., & Sanders, M. (2008). The efficacy of the Triple P-Positive parenting program in improving parenting and child behavior: A comparison with two other treatment conditions. *Behaviour Research and Therapy, 46*(4), 411–427.

Bronfenbrenner, U. (1979). *The ecology of human development: Experiments by nature and design.* Cambridge, MA: Harvard University Press.

Bronfenbrenner, U. (2005). Growing chaos in the lives of children, youth, and families: How can we turn it around. In U. Bronfenbrenner (Ed.), *Making human beings human: Bioecological perspectives on human development* (pp. 185–197). Thousand Oaks, CA: Sage.

Bronfenbrenner, U., & Morris, P. (2006). The ecology of developmental processes. In W. Damon & R. Lerner (Eds.), *Handbook of child psychology* (pp. 993–1028). New York: Wiley.

Brooks-Gunn, J., Fuligni, A.S., & Berlin, L.J. (2003). *Early child development in the 21st century : Profiles of current research initiatives.* New York, London: Teachers College Press.

Bruer, J.T. (1999). *The myth of the first three years*. New York: The Free Press.

Campbell, F.A., & Ramey, C.T. (1994). Effects of early intervention on intellectual and academic achievement: A follow-up study of children from low-income families. *Child Development, 65*, 684–698.

Campbell, F.A., & Ramey, C.T. (1995). Cognitive and school outcomes for high-risk African-American students at middle adolescence: Positive effects of early intervention. *American Educational Research Journal, 32*(4), 743–772.

Campbell, F.A., Ramey, C.T., Pungello, E., Sparling, J., & Miller-Johnson, S. (2002). Early childhood education: Young adult outcomes from the Abecedarian Project. *Applied Developmental Science, 6*(1), 42–57.

Caspi, A., Henry, B., McGee, R., Moffitt, T., & Silva, P. (1995). Temperamental origins of child and adolescent behavior problems: From age three to age fifteen. *Child Development, 66*(1), 55–68.

Cohen, N., & Radford, J. (1999). *The impact of early childhood intervention on later life*. Toronto, Canada: Hincks-Dellcrest Institute.

Coie, J. (1996). Prevention of violence and antisocial behavior. In R. Peters & R. McMahon (Eds.), *Preventing childhood disorders, substance abuse, and delinquency* (Vol. 3, pp. 1–18). London: Sage Publications.

Coie, J., Terry, R., Lenox, K., Lochman, J., & Hyman, C. (1995). Childhood peer rejection and aggression as predictors of stable patterns of adolescent disorder. *Development and Psychopathology, 7*(4), 697–713.

Conger, R., Conger, K., Elder, G., Lorenz, F., Simons, R., & Whitbeck, L. (1993). Family economic stress and adjustment of early adolescent girls. *Developmental Psychology, 29*(2), 206–219.

Das, C. (2010). Resilience, risk and protective factors for British-Indian children of divorce. *Journal of Social Science, 25*(1–2–3), 97–108.

Diener, E., Suh, E., & Oishi, S. (1997). Recent findings on subjective well-being. *Indian Journal of Clinical Psychology, 24*(1), 25–41.

Dishion, T., Capaldi, D., Spracklen, K., & Li, F. (1995). Peer ecology of male adolescent drug use. *Development and Psychopathology, 7*(4), 803–824.

Eckenrode, J., Ganzel, B., Henderson, C.R., Smith, E., Olds, D., Powers, J., . . . Sidora, K. (2000). Preventing child abuse and neglect with a program of nurse home visitation. *JAMA, 284*(11), 1385–1391.

Elder, G. (1998). The life course as developmental theory. *Child Development, 69*(1), 1–12.

Farrington, D. (1994). Early developmental prevention of juvenile delinquency. *RSA Journal, 142*(5454), 22–34.

Farrington, D., Coid, J., & Murray, J. (2009). Family factors in the intergenerational transmission of offending. *Criminal Behaviour and Mental Health, 19*(2), 109–124.

Farrington, D., & Welsh, B.C. (2003). Family-based prevention of offending: A meta-analysis. *The Australian and New Zealand Journal of Criminology, 36*(2), 127–151.

Febbraro, A. (1994). Single mothers "at risk" for child maltreatment: An appraisal of person centred interventions and a call for emancipatory action. *Canadian Journal of Community Mental Health, 13*(2), 47–60.

Felner, R., Brand, S., DuBois, D., Adan, A., Mulhall, P., & Evans, E. (1995). Socioeconomic disadvantage, proximal environmental experiences, and socioemotional and academic adjustment in early adolescence: Investigation of a mediated effects model. *Child Development, 66*(3), 774–792.

Fergusson, D., Swain-Campbell, N., & Horwood, J. (2004). How does childhood economic disadvantage lead to crime? *Journal of Child Psychology and Psychiatry, 45*(5), 956–966.

Franklin, K. (2014). Mental illness and crime. In G. Bruinsma & D. Weisburd (Eds.), *The encyclopedia of criminology and criminal justice* (pp. 1–8). New York: Springer Science Business Media.

Freiberg, K., Homel, R., & Branch, S. (2010). Circles of care: The struggle to strengthen child developmental systems though the pathways to prevention project. *Family Matters, 84*(1), 28–34.

GHK Consulting – Holden McAllister Partnership and IPSOS Public Affairs. (2004). *The riintegration of children absent, excluded or missing from school.* Nottingham: DfES Publications.

Gordon, R.S.J. (1983). An operational classification of disease prevention. *Public Health Reports, 98*(2), 107–109.

Gray, S.W., & Klaus, R.A. (1970). The early training project: A seventh-year report. *Child Development, 41*(4), 909–924.

Hayes, A. (2006). Maintaining the gains: Sustainability in prevention and early intervention. *Family Matters, 75*, 66–69.

Heckman, J. (2015). *4 Big benefits of investing in early childhood development.* Retrieved from http://heckmanequation.org/content/4-big-benefits-investing-early-childhood-development.

Heckman, J., Stixrud, J., & Urzua, S. (2006). The effects of cognitive and non-cognitive abilities on labour market outcomes and social behaviour. *Journal of Labour Economics, 24*(3), 411–482.

Hertzman, C. (1999). The biological embedding of early experience and its effects on health in adulthood. *Annals of the New York Academy of Sciences, 896*(1), 85–95.

Hirschi, T. (1994). Family. In T. Hirschi & M. Gottfredson (Eds.), *The generality* of *deviance* (pp. 47–69). New Brunswick, NJ: Transaction Publishers.

Hirschi, T., & Gottfredson, M. (1994). The generality of deviance. In E. McLaughlin & J. Muncie (Eds.), *Criminological perspectives: Essential readings* (3rd ed.) (pp. 23–47). New Brunswick, NJ: Transaction Publishers.

Hockfield, S., & Lombroso, P. (1998). Development of the cerebral cortex: IX. Cortical development and experience: I. *Journal of American Academic Child Adolescence Psychiatry, 37*(9), 992–993. Retrieved from http://info.med.yale.edu/chldstdy/plomdevelop/development/september.html.

Homel, R. (2005). Developmental crime prevention. In N. Tilley (Ed.), *Handbook of crime prevention and community safety* (pp. 71–106). Cullompton, Devon: Willan Publishing.

Homel, R., Elias, G., & Hay, I. (2001). Developmental prevention in a disadvantaged community. In R. Eckersley, J. Dixon & B. Douglas (Eds.), *The social origins of health and well-being* (pp. 269–278). Cambridge: Cambridge University Press.

Homel, R., Freiberg, K., Lamb, C., Leech, M., Carr, A., Hampshire, A., . . . Batchelor, S. (2006). *The pathways to prevention project: The first five years 1999–2004.* Brisbane: Griffith University and Mission Australia.

Hubbell, V., McKey, R., Condelli, L., Ganson, H., Barrett, B., McConkey, C., & Plantz, M. (1985). *The impact of Head Start on children, families and communities: Head start synthesis project.* Washington, DC: DHHS Publication.

Huh, D., Tristan, J., Wade, E., & Stice, E. (2006). Does problem behavior elicit poor parenting? A prospective study of adolescent girls. *Journal of Adolescent Research, 21*(2), 185–204.

Johnson, D.L. (2006). Parent-child development center follow-up project: Child behaviour problem results. *The Journal of Primary Prevention, 27*(4), 391–407.

Johnson, D.L., & Blumenthal, J.B. (2004). The parent-child development centers and school achievement: A follow-up. *The Journal of Primary Prevention, 25*(2), 195–209.

Karoly, L., Greenwood, P., Everingham, S.S., Hoube, J., Kilburn, M.R., Rydell, C.P., . . . Chiesa, J. (1998). *Investing in our children: What we know and don't know about the costs and benefits of early childhood interventions.* Santa Monica, CA: RAND.

Keating, D.P., & Hertzman, C. (1999). Modernity's paradox. In D.P. Keating & C. Hertzman (Eds.), *Developmental health and the wealth of nations: Social, biological and educational dynamics* (pp. 1–18). New York: The Guilford Press.

Knudson, E., Heckman, J., Cameron, J., & Shonkoff, J. (2006). *Economic, neuro-biological, and behavioral perspectives on building America's future workforce.* Paper presented at the National Academy of Sciences.

Lally, R.J., Mangione, P.L., & Honig, A.S. (1988). The Syracuse University family development research program: Long-range impact on an early intervention with low-income children and their families. In D.R. Powell (Ed.), *Parent education as early childhood intervention: Emerging directions in theory, research and practice* (Vol. 3, pp. 79–104). Norwood, NJ: Ablex Publishing Corporation.

Laub, J.H., & Sampson, R.J. (2005). A general age-graded theory of crime: Lessons learned and the future of life-course criminology. In D. Farrington (Ed.), *Advances in criminological theory, Volume 13: Testing integrated developmental/life course theories of offending* (165–182). New Brunswick, NJ: Transaction Publishers.

Lazar, I., & Darlington, R. (1982). Lasting effects of early education: A report from the consortium for longitudinal studies. *Monographs of the Society for Research in Child Development, 47*(2–3), 1–151.

Lerner, R. (2006). Developmental science, developmental systems, and contemporary theories of human development. *Handbook of Child Psychology, 1: Theoretical Models of Human Development, 1,* 1–17.

Lerner, R. (2012). Developmental science: Past, present, and future. *International Journal of Developmental Science, 6*(1–2), 29–36.

Lerner, R., & Overton, W. (2008). Exemplifying the integrations of the relational developmental system. *Journal of Adolescent Research, 23*(3), 245–255.

Levenstein, P., Levenstein, S., Shiminski, J.A., & Stolzberg, J.E. (1998). Long-term impact of a verbal interaction program for at-risk toddlers: An exploratory study of high school outcomes in a replication of the Mother-Child Home Program. *Journal of Applied Developmental Psychology, 19*(2), 267–285.

Little, M. (1999). Prevention and early intervention with children in need: Definitions, principles and examples of good practice. *Children and Society, 13,* 304–316.

Lynam, D., Moffitt, T., & Stouthamer-Loeber, M. (1993). Explaining the relation between IQ and delinquency: Class, race, test motivation, school failure, or self-control? *Journal of Abnormal Psychology, 102*(2), 187.

MacLeod, J., & Nelson, G. (2000). Programs for the promotion of family wellness and the prevention of child maltreatment: A meta-analytic review. *Child Abuse and Neglect, 24*(9), 1127–1149.

Manning, M. (2004). *Measuring the costs of community-based developmental prevention programs in Australia.* (Masters (Hons)), Griffith University, Brisbane.

Manning, M. (2008). *Economic evaluation of the effects of early childhood intervention programs on adolescent outcomes.* (PhD), Griffith University, Brisbane.

Manning, M., Homel, R., & Smith, C. (2010). A meta-analysis of the effects of early developmental prevention programs in at-risk populations on non-health outcomes in adolescence. *Children and Youth Services Review, 32*(4), 506–519.

Matsueda, R., & Anderson, K. (1998). The dynamics of delinquent peers and delinquent behavior. *Criminology, 36*(2), 269–308.

McCain, M.N., Mustard, F.J., Coffey, C., Gordon, M., Comis, J., Offord, D., . . . Williams, R. (1999). *Early years study: Reversing the real brain – final report.* Ontario: Ontario Children's Secretariat.

McLoyd, V.C. (1998). Children in poverty: Development, public policy, and practice. In W. Damon, I.E. Sigel, & K.A. Renniger (Eds.), *Handbook of child psychology* (Vol. 4: Child psychology in practice), (pp. 135–208). New York: John Wiley and Sons.

Meisels, S., & Shonkoff, J. (2000). Early childhood intervention: A continuing evolution. In S. Meisels & J. Shonkoff (Eds.), *Handbook of early childhood intervention* (pp. 3–31). New York: Cambridge University Press.

Meyer, L.A. (1984). Long-term academic effects of the direct instruction project follow through. *The Elementary School Journal, 84*(4), 380–394.

Miller, L., & Bizzell, R.P. (1983). Long-term effects of four preschool programs: Sixth, seventh, and eighth grades. *Child Development, 54*(3), 727–741.

Moffitt, T. (1990). Juvenile delinquency and attention deficit disorder: Boys' developmental trajectories from age 3 to age 15. *Child Development, 61*(3), 893–910.

Moffitt, T. (1993a). Adolescence-limited and life-course-persistent antisocial behavior: A developmental taxonomy. *Psychological Review, 100*(4), 674.

Moffitt, T. (1993b). The neuropsychology of conduct disorder. *Development and Psychopathology, 5*(1–2), 135–151.

Nelson, G., Westhues, A., Laurier, W., & MacLeod, J. (2003). A meta-analysis of longitudinal research on preschool prevention programs for children. *Prevention and Treatment, 6*, 1–35.

O'Malley, K. (2015). Alcohol-related neurodevelopmental disorder. In I. Stolerman & L. Price (Eds.), *Encyclopedia of Psychopharmacology* (pp. 83–91). Berlin: Springer-Verlag.

Olds, D. (1988). The prenatal/early infancy project. In R. Price, E. Cowen, R. Lorion, & J. Ramos-McKay (Eds.), *Fourteen ounces of prevention: A casebook for practitioners* (pp. 9–23). Washington, DC: American Psychological Association.

Olds, D. (2002). Prenatal and infancy home visiting by nurses: From randomized trials to community replication. *Prevention Science, 3*(3), 153–172.

Olds, D., Henderson, C., Chamberlin, R., & Tatelbaum, R. (1986). Preventing child abuse and neglect: A randomized trial of nurse home visitation. *Pediatrics, 78*(1), 65–78.

Olds, D., Henderson, C.R., Cole, R., Eckenrode, J., Kitzman, H., Luckey, D., . . . Powers, J. (1998). Long-term effects of nurse home visitation on children's criminal and antisocial behaviour. *Journal of the American Medical Association, 280*(14), 1238–1244.

Olds, D., Henderson, C., Kitzman, H., Eckenrode, J., Cole, R., & Tatelbaum, R. (1999). Prenatal and infancy home visitation by nurses: Recent findings. *The Future of Children, 9*(1), 44–65.

Olds, D., Hill, P., & Ramsey, E. (1998). *Prenatal and early childhood nurse home visitation*. Washington, DC: US Department of Justice, Office of Justice Programs, Office of Juvenile Justice and Delinquency Prevention.

Olds, D., Kitzman, H., Cole, R., & Robinson, J. (1997). Theoretical foundations of a program of home visitation for pregnant women and parents of young children. *Journal of Community Psychology, 25*(1), 9–25.

Olds, D., & Korfmacher, J. (1997). The evolution of a program of research on prenatal and early childhood home visitation: Special issue introduction. *Journal of Community Psychology, 25*(1), 1–7.

Popper, K. (1959). *The logic of scientific discovery*. London: Hutchinson.

Ramey, C.T., & Landesman Ramey, S. (1998). Early intervention and early experience. *American Psychologist, 53*(2), 109–120.

Rankin, J., & Kern, R. (1994). Parental attachments and delinquency. *Criminology, 32*(4), 495–515.

Reynolds, A.J. (1994). Effects of a preschool plus follow-on intervention for children at-risk. *Developmental Psychology, 30*(6), 787–804.

Reynolds, A.J., Temple, J.A., Robertson, D.L., & Mann, E.A. (2001). Long-term effects of an early childhood intervention on educational achievement and juvenile arrest: A 15 year follow-up of low income children in public school. *Journal of the American Medical Association, 285*(18), 2339–2346.

Rodning, C., Beckwith, L., & Howard, J. (1989). Characteristics of attachment organization and play organization in prenatally drug-exposed toddlers. *Development and Psychopathology, 1*(4), 277–289.

Rutter, M. (2000). Resilience considered: Conceptual considerations, empirical findings, and policy implications. In J. Shonkoff & S. Meisels (Eds.), *Handbook of early childhood intervention* (2nd ed., pp. 651–682). New York: Cambridge University Press.

Rutter, M. (2007). Sure start local programmes: An outsider's perspective. In J. Belsky, J. Barnes, & E. Melhuish (Eds.), *The national evaluation of sure start: Does area-based early intervention work?* (pp. 197–210). Bristol: The Policy Press: The University of Bristol.

Sampson, R., & Laub, J. (1990). Crime and deviance over the life course: The salience of adult social bonds. *American Sociological Review, 55*, 609–627.

Sanson, A., Smart, D., Prior, M., & Oberklaid, F. (1993). Precursors of hyperactivity and aggression. *Journal of the American Academy of Child & Adolescent Psychiatry, 32*(6), 1207–1216.

Sen, A., & Nussbaum, M. (1996). Functioing and capability: The foundation of Sen's and Nussbaum's development of ethic. *Political Theory, 24*(4), 584–612.

Sokol, R., Delaney-Black, V., & Nordstrom, B. (2003). Fetal alcohol spectrum disorder. *JAMA, 290*(22), 2996–2999.

Sprigle, J.E., & Schaefer, L. (1985). Longitudinal evaluation of the effects of two compensatory preschool programs on fourth- through sixth-grade students. *Developmental Psychology, 21*(4), 702–708.

Stanley, F., Richardson, S., & Prior, M. (2005). *Children of the lucky country? How Australia has turned its back on children and why children matter*. Sydney: Pan Macmillan.

Steinberg, L. (2009). Adolescent development and juvenile justice. *Annual Review of Clinical Psychology, 5*, 459–485.

Straus, M., Gelles, R., & Smith, C. (1990). *Physical violence in American families: Risk factors and adaptations to violence in 8,145 families*. New Brunswick, NJ: Transaction Publishers.

The World Health Organisation. (1999). Health and development in the 20th century. In *The world health report – making a difference* (pp. 1–12). Geneva, Switzerland.

White, J., Moffitt, T., Caspi, A., Bartusch, D., Needles, D., & Stouthamer-Loeber, M. (1994). Measuring impulsivity and examining its relationship to delinquency. *Journal of Abnormal Psychology, 103*(2), 192.

Wikstrom, P., & Loeber, R. (2000). Do disadvantaged neighborhoods cause well-adjusted children to become adolescent delinquents-a study of male juvenile serious offending, individual risk and protective factors, and neighborhood context. *Criminology, 38*(4), 1109–1142.

Chapter 6

Closing the educational gap between mainstream and Indigenous children

Indigenous children in Australia (0 to 14 years of age) make up approximately one-third of the Indigenous population. The population is relatively young with a very large proportion of the population aged between 0–24 years (Biddle, 2012). This group has poor prospects with respect to their education, employment and health. Moreover, many children/youth (aged 0–14 and 15–24 years, respectively) will be caught up, either directly through their own involvement or indirectly through the involvement of a family member, in alcohol and drug abuse, domestic violence and crime.

Unfortunately, the history of policies concerning Indigenous Australians is awash with unintended outcomes. Despite considerable investment from all levels of government, many outcomes for Indigenous Australians are not improving and, for those that are, there is still a considerable way to go to achieve the Council of Australian Governments' commitment to 'closing the gap' on Indigenous disadvantage. For example, evidence shows little change in literacy, numeracy, most health indicators and housing overcrowding for Indigenous people. Moreover, rates of child abuse and neglect substantiations and adult imprisonment have increased (Council of Australian Governments, 2012).

With respect to education, the recent release of the Prime Minister's (2016) report on closing the gap on Indigenous disadvantage shows mixed results. In summary, progress on the target to halve the gap in reading and numeracy for Indigenous students by 2018 appears to be on track. Across the eight areas (reading and numeracy for Years 3, 5, 7 and 9), the proportion of Aboriginal and Torres Strait Islander students achieving national minimum standards is on track in four of these eight areas. Clearly, however, only meeting the target in four areas does highlight the need to consolidate our efforts to meet this goal. Another important area is the 2014 COAG target to close the gap in school attendance by the end of 2018. 2015 results show that the attendance rate for Aboriginal and Torres Strait Islander students was 83.7 per cent, little change from the rate in 2014 (83.5 per cent). It is obvious that progress will need to accelerate for this target to be met.

The salient questions are: (1) How can we close the educational gap between Indigenous and non-Indigenous children in a meaningful and sustainable way?

120 Closing the educational gap

(2) Can education break the vicious cycle that Indigenous people face in rural and remote communities? In particular, can education assist in overcoming the overwhelming feeling of hopelessness, discrimination, alcoholism, drug abuse, domestic violence and crime that currently affect Indigenous people and communities? In this chapter we attempt to provide some evidence that will assist policy makers unpack the complexity of this issue and potentially provide some links to educational, economic and developmental literatures that will assist in developing solutions to answer these complex and difficult questions.

The chapter begins by examining the state of Indigenous early education in Australia. Next, we look at key trends with respect to: (1) the decision to participate in ECEC services; (2) school readiness and ECEC participation; (3) developmental vulnerability, mental health and ECEC participation; and (4) cognitive, behavioral outcomes and ECEC participation. We then discuss the importance of quality ECEC services and staff retention and the necessary partnerships to achieve ECEC policy goals before, finally, making some recommendations regarding the potential solutions – namely, educational, economic and developmental (discussed in earlier chapters).

The state of affairs of Indigenous early childhood education and care (ECEC) in Australia

The initial 'Closing the Gap' target aimed to ensure access to early childhood education and care (ECEC) services for all Indigenous four-year-olds in remote communities by 2013. A new, expanded target has been devised to provide ECEC access for 95 per cent of all Indigenous children by 2025 (Department of the Prime Minister and Cabinet, 2016). Importantly, ensuring ECEC access and participation for all Indigenous children has gained significant position in Australia's national as well as state and local policy agendas. This policy impetus has been accompanied by legislative changes to improve the quality of ECEC services (i.e. the National Quality Framework or NQF),[1] as well as by proposed reforms to extend government subsidies to private ECEC providers (Productivity Commission, 2014).

While the developmental gains from participating in high-quality ECEC services have been confirmed by international as well as Australian population-wide studies (see Chapters 4 and 5), research on the effects of ECEC participation for Indigenous children is more limited. Further, there is a high level of uncertainty with regard to measuring the progress of 'Closing the Gap' targets, as administrative data that is used to make these estimates is often outdated. With the advent of the Longitudinal Study of Indigenous Children (LSIC) (Australian Government, 2016) and other Indigenous-specific data (e.g. NATSISS (see Australian Bureau of Statistics, 2015)), researchers have been able to draw important lessons on how ECEC affects a nationally representative sample of Indigenous children and families. It should be noted, however, that these studies are recent and important relevant questions to the development of Indigenous policy in Australia remain unanswered.

Important data: the Longitudinal Study of Indigenous Children (LSIC)

LSIC aims to capture data that will improve our understanding of issues faced (e.g. health, education, employment, drug addiction, criminal justice) by Aboriginal and Torres Strait Islander children, their families and communities. It is anticipated that these data and the studies that employ these data will improve policy responses to issues regarding the quality of life of Indigenous Australians. LSIC provides quantitative and qualitative data that can be used to provide a better insight into how a child's early years affect their development. LSIC collects information about parenting, family relationships, childhood education, child and parent health, as well as culture and community. LSIC began in 2008 with two groups of Aboriginal and/or Torres Strait Islander children aged 0 to 18 months and three and a half to five years. Over 1,680 families were interviewed in Wave 1. LSCI is longitudinal and as such interviews are carried out annually, with more than 1,200 parents and children followed up in each subsequent wave (Australian Government, 2016).

Key Trends and Findings

The decision to participate in ECEC services

Overall, more children are entering ECEC in Australia than ever before. However, there are a number of individuals within the Australian population who are less likely to participate fully in ECEC services. These include children from low-income families, those families who live in remote areas, Indigenous children, those from non-English speaking backgrounds, refugees and new migrants as well as those children with special health needs (Gilley, Tayler, Niklas, & Cloney, 2015). While both Indigenous children and those children from non-English speaking backgrounds are significantly less likely to attend school, non-attendance for Indigenous children is higher than for the latter group (Brennan & Adamson, 2014). Figure 6.1 clearly shows that some groups are under-represented in ECEC in Australia.

Recent Productivity Commission (2016) data show:

- An increase in children under five attending ECEC services – up from 34 per cent in 2006 to 43 per cent in 2014;
- That Aboriginal and Torres Strait children make up approximately 5.5 per cent of all 0–5-year-olds but only account for 2.2 per cent of ECEC participants;

122 Closing the educational gap

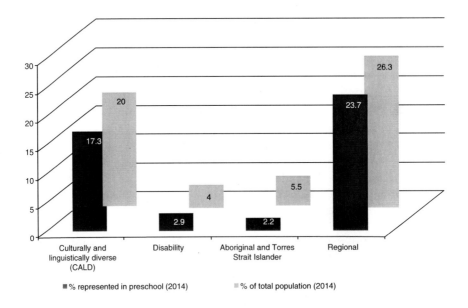

Figure 6.1 Percentage of 0–5-Year-Olds in ECEC Services in Australia
Data derived from O'Conner et al. (2016)

- That children with a disability make up approximately 4 per cent of all 0–5-year-olds but only account for 2.9 per cent of ECEC participants;
- That children from regional areas make up approximately 26.3 per cent of all 0–5-year-olds but only account for 23.7 per cent of ECEC participants; and
- Children from culturally and linguistically diverse backgrounds (CALD) make up approximately 20 per cent of all 0–5-year-olds but only account for 11.1 per cent of ECEC participants.

The participation of Indigenous children in ECEC is of great importance given the levels of disadvantage in their communities. Most developmental scholars would agree that intervention is most successful when targeted to those individuals most in need (Heckman, 2006; Manning, 2008, 2014). A large proportion of Aboriginal and Torres Strait Islander children who participate in ECEC services are enrolled in mainstream services that cater to both non-Indigenous and Indigenous children (Productivity Commission, 2011). The real issue is that those children most at risk require additional services above those for mainstream children. Mainstream services attempt to work closely and productively with Indigenous families and communities, but due to no fault of their own (often lack of training and specialised funding) do not provide the full suite of services that are required for this population. As a consequence, Indigenous children may not be afforded the same quality (in terms of meeting their needs) of early education as mainstream children (Productivity Commission, 2011).

Quality of the ECEC experience may be one factor that explains low attendance rates for Indigenous children. But there are probably others. O'Conner et al. (2016) utilise two consecutive samples from the Australian Early Development Census data to understand the factors that determine non-attendance at ECEC programs for various subgroups of Australian children, as well as to see how non-attendance has evolved over the 2008–2011 period. The authors find that at both census points, Indigenous status, coming from a non-English speaking background, as well as living in a disadvantaged area, all led to significantly higher odds of non-attendance at preschool, even after controlling for a range of observable characteristics. The size of the odds ratio was similar for being Indigenous and coming from a non-English-speaking background, while the odds of preschool non-attendance was largest for children coming from the most socio-economically disadvantaged areas. When accounting for other covariates, children living in remote communities had the same odds in 2008 (or higher odds in 2011) of attending ECEC as did children in urban areas. These results are supported by Baxter and Hand (2013), who use various Australian surveys to find the odd ratios of ECEC attendance. Being from an Indigenous or non-English speaking background led to lower ECEC participation, and the odds ratio of participation is smaller for these two subgroups than it is for children with special health needs. These results hold across most states and territories in Australia, with significant determinants of ECEC participation varying greatly by Indigenous status.

Indeed, the low participation rates among Indigenous children are largely explained by family- and community-level characteristics, such as Indigenous families having lower household incomes, lower parental educational attainment and higher chances of living in remote areas where it is more difficult to provide quality ECEC services (Baxter & Hand, 2013). These results reinforce the findings of Biddle (2007), who shows that the lower levels of ECEC attendance for Indigenous children can be largely explained by lower household incomes, lower parental education levels and higher incidence of geographic disadvantage.

Grace, Bowes, and Elcombe (2014) undertook a study on ECEC participation using data from 101 disadvantaged families in New South Wales, of which 17 were Indigenous families. They examined the factors that support or hinder ECEC participation. Rather interestingly, they found that quality and not cost was a key restricting factor noted by families (including Indigenous families) with respect to ECEC participation. Of all groups of families in the sample (groups were created based on location or cultural background) only Indigenous carers viewed 'staff having my same ethnicity' as a facilitator to ECEC participation, highlighting the importance of employing Indigenous staff in order to engage Indigenous families and promote Indigenous culture and values.

Using LSIC data to analyse the determinants of ECEC participation, Hewitt and Walter (2014) found that geographic remoteness, household income (with the exception of receiving welfare, which led to a negative effect on ECEC

124 Closing the educational gap

participation), and the characteristics of the primary care, all had little effect on the probability of attending ECEC. Conversely, stability of housing (i.e. little household mobility), having access to learning resources (e.g. books), children having relatively easy access to health services thus having better health, and not concerned about child learning ECEC material, all had a positive and significant relationship with ECEC participation among Indigenous children.

School readiness and ECEC participation

School readiness relates to the ability of children, as well as their family, community and educators to possess qualities at the start of school that support higher educational achievement at later stages in their formal schooling. Mixed-method research points to the importance of employing Indigenous staff (and non-Indigenous staff formally trained in culturally inclusive methods) to help Indigenous parents build trust in formal education, as well as understand how they can help enhance the learning experience of their children (Dockett, Perry, & Kearney, 2010). There is also evidence to show that involving Indigenous communities in the school, for example, celebrating Indigenous culture, enhances the learning experience of Indigenous children. This is especially important given the priority on ECEC access at the policy level. In reality, access is not sufficient to ensure participation in programs by Indigenous families in the case when they perceive the ECEC centers as not meeting their needs. Hewitt and Walter (2014) argue, children's school readiness is also influenced by the school's readiness for the children, demonstrated by valuing Indigenous staff and providing a positive welcoming environment for families. Trudgett and Grace (2011) conducted a qualitative study that reinforces the importance of trust that Indigenous mothers place on the ECEC providers, especially in terms of respecting and embracing Indigenous culture. Similarly, Biddle (2007) conducted a quantitative study on the determinants of ECEC attendance for Indigenous children, also finding that the presence of Indigenous school staff significantly increased the probability of attendance.

Beyond access to quality ECEC services, ensuring that lessons are culturally appropriate should be a key focus of ECEC programs aimed at engaging Indigenous families. Evidence shows us that culturally responsive formal education enhances not only standard measures of achievement but also Indigenous-specific measures of wellbeing (Dockery, 2011; Miller, 2004). Yet, Indigenous families often worry about the loss of Indigenous culture that can occur when children are exposed to Western-style education. However, it should be noted that incorporating Indigenous-specific skills into formal education has been shown to be an effective way of passing on important Indigenous skills and values (see Reyes-García et al., 2010). Savage et al. (2011) explain how, for the case of New Zealand, low school attendance for Maori students has been linked to students feeling that the school's culture is disparate from their own. Conversely, schools in New Zealand that effectively implemented culturally inclusive curricula, saw strong improvements in the test scores of students (Bishop et al., 2012). Although this study was carried out for secondary school students, it highlights the potential gains that can be made for Indigenous students' performance by implementing culturally inclusive programs at younger ages.

Dockett et al. (2010) reviewed school readiness as it related to Australia's Indigenous peoples. They argue that curricula and standardised tests designed for non-Indigenous children disadvantage Indigenous children both in terms of the learning experience, as well as by reinforcing the view that they are lagging behind non-Indigenous children by not acknowledging their skills and strengths. An example of this can be seen in study results that measure literacy in English, when many Indigenous children are proficient mainly or exclusively in an Indigenous language. Furthermore, the authors claim that viewing Indigenous peoples as a single group fails to recognise the diversity among Indigenous communities, which have arguably different needs.

McTurk et al. (2011) build on Dockett, Perry and Kearney's findings regarding school readiness by explaining that one of the culturally appropriate teaching strategies that may enhance educational outcomes includes one where Indigenous education utilises outdoor environments. The importance of this setting is that Indigenous children feel comfortable and closely identify with an outdoor setting. As Preston et al. (2012) explain: "for Aboriginal peoples, learning is a lived experience best absorbed through activities such as storytelling, group discussions, cooperative learning, demonstrations, role modeling, personal reflection, peer tutoring, learning circles, talking circles and hands-on experiences" (p. 9). These results are stressed as well by Purdie et al. (2011), who explain that in some Indigenous communities, young children are often exposed to two Indigenous languages associated to various dialects as well as to a variety of signs and gestures, but that they are rarely exposed to English. Clearly, Indigenous experts are consistently skeptical of mainstream tests that have not been validated for Indigenous children, and which are rarely systematically adopted to study the effects of ECEC on a representative sample of Indigenous children. Although the Longitudinal Study of Indigenous Children (LSIC) has the advantage of incorporating standardised tests specifically validated for Indigenous children, these tests are still unable to capture competence in Indigenous-specific skills, which is an important determinant of Indigenous wellbeing (Dockett et al., 2010).

Developmental vulnerability, mental health and ECEC participation

Approximately 20 per cent of Australian children entering ECEC (kindergarten) are developmentally vulnerable in one or more of the Australian Early Development Census domains (Table 6.1). These statistics are higher for children living in disadvantaged communities (32 per cent) and higher again for Indigenous children (43.2 per cent) (McKenzie & Da Costa, 2015). Clearly, focusing on ECEC participation for these subgroups of Australian children and families is critical in order to decrease the developmental vulnerability of Australia's disadvantaged children.

Table 6.1 AECD Domains and Sub-Domains

Domain	Sub-domain	Description
Physical health and wellbeing	Physical readiness for the school day	Whether the child is dressed appropriately for school activities, comes to school on time, and is not hungry or tired
	Physical independence	Whether the child is independent regarding their own needs, has an established hand preference and is well coordinated
	Gross and fine motor skills	Child's ability to physically tackle the school day, including gross and fine motor skills
Social competence	Overall social competence	Overall social development, including the ability to get along and play with other children, cooperativeness and self-confidence
	Responsibility and respect	Whether child shows respect for others and for property, follows rules, takes care of materials, accepts responsibility for actions, and shows self-control
	Approaches to learning	Whether child works neatly and independently, can solve problems, follow instructions and class routines, and easily adjust to changes
	Readiness to explore new things	Whether child is curious about the surrounding world, and eager to explore new books, toys or unfamiliar objects and games
Emotional maturity	Prosocial and helping behaviour	Whether child shows helping behaviours including helping someone hurt, sick or upset, offering to help spontaneously, and inviting others to join in
	Anxious and fretful behaviour	Whether child shows anxious behaviours, is happy and able to enjoy school, and is comfortable being left at school

Domain	Sub-domain	Description
	Aggressive behaviour	Whether child shows aggressive behaviours as a means of solving a conflict and has temper tantrums
	Hyperactivity and inattention	Hyperactive behaviors and ability to concentrate, settle to chosen activities, wait their turn, and think before acting
Language and cognitive development	Basic literacy	Basic literacy skills including how to handle a book, ability to identify some letters and attach sounds to some letters, show awareness of rhyming words, know the writing directions, and ability to write their own name
	Interest in literacy/numeracy and memory	Interest in books and reading, math and numbers, and memory functioning
	Advanced literacy	Advanced literacy skills such as reading simple words or sentences, and writing simple words or sentences
	Basic numeracy	Basic numeracy skills such as counting to 20, recognising shapes and numbers, comparing numbers, sorting and classifying, use of one-to-one correspondence, and understanding simple time concepts
Communication skills and general knowledge	Communication skills and general knowledge	Ability to communicate easily and effectively, participate in storytelling or imaginative play, articulate clearly and show adequate standard knowledge

Source: Goldfeld et al. (2015)

Harrison et al. (2012) outline the effect of ECEC programs on Indigenous children, noting that while most Indigenous children are on track in most of the Australian Early Development Index (AEDI) domains, there are still a number of children who are vulnerable with respect to language and cognitive skills. The authors emphasise the importance of culturally responsive Indigenous-specific programs in enhancing children's outcomes. This does not only include ensuring the culture of Indigenous children is respected, but also embraced – Indigenous

128 Closing the educational gap

families seek services that actively try and allow their children to remain skilled in Indigenous-specific capabilities (Colbung et al., 2007). Harrison et al. (2012) argue that while mixed methods studies exist, they often lack the ability to account rigorously for baseline characteristics or to have enough observations to verify qualitative insights. For Australian evidence see Moss et al. (2015). For evidence of Canada's Headstart program see Preston et al. (2012).

A primary goal regarding ECEC policy in Australia is ensuring that Indigenous children in remote communities have access to quality ECEC services. Nutton (2013) and Nutton et al. (2011) examine the effectiveness of mobile ECEC (preschool) services for very remote Indigenous communities. Mobile ECEC services were designed to provide training to local Indigenous people to deliver ECEC services themselves while under the support and supervision of trained ECEC teachers. Nutton's (2013) study " . . . evaluated the extent to which children's participation in the innovative Mobile Preschool Program improved school readiness outcomes in comparison with children who did not participate and those who had limited exposure to the program" (p. ii). In short, Nutton's study quantified the effects of program availability, attendance and quality on follow-up measures of development and school readiness using the Australian Early Development Index (AEDI). Results point to a substantial improvement in the AEDI scores for children aged 3–5 years who consistently participated in the program over a school year. These gains translated to participating children being substantially less likely to be developmentally vulnerable.

Crucially, Australia also needs to further explore the mental wellbeing of Indigenous families and children. We need to be able to answer the question: how does a child's mental wellbeing or the mental wellbeing of their parents or caregivers affect Indigenous participation in ECEC? To date, there is very little robust evidence that analyses the mental health of young Indigenous children and their families at a nationally representative level. The best source, to date, is a study from Western Australia, which focused on Indigenous children aged 4–17 years of age (De Maio et al., 2005). Results reveal that about 25 per cent per cent of children in the study exhibited serious emotional and behavioral disorders. The percentage of those who present with serious disorders was much higher for Indigenous than non-Indigenous children (about 15 per cent vs. 25 per cent). Most worrisome is the fact that the rates of serious behavioral and emotional difficulties are higher among 4–11-year-olds, which provides some evidence of the importance of addressing the mental health of Indigenous families and children early in life (as discussed in Chapter 4).

Cognitive, behavioral outcomes and ECEC participation

Internationally, ECEC programs have consistently shown that the gains of participation are non-linear, with developmentally vulnerable children (e.g. at-risk and minority students), making the strongest test score gains from ECEC participation in the short-term, while long-term gains occurred mostly when programs begin at very young ages (Barnett, 1998; Boocock, 1995). Quality ECEC programs that focus almost exclusively on improving the outcomes of disadvantaged children have also shown gains lasting well into adulthood (Nores et al., 2005). More recently, Camilli et al. (2010), Manning (2008), and Manning, Homel, and Smith (2010) conducted meta-analyses on the effect of ECEC programs on children's outcomes in the short and long terms. Consistently, the studies find evidence of ECEC boosting the behavioral outcomes in children, with improved social and emotional outcomes lasting beyond childhood. Manning et al. (2010) find evidence of improvements to educational outcomes (namely educational success (d = 0.53) and cognitive development (d = 0.34)), family functioning (d = 0.18), reductions in social deviance (d = 0.48) and reductions in involvement with the criminal justice system (d = 0.24) during the adolescent years.

One key qualification that applies to ECEC participation in Australia and most Western countries is the detrimental effect that spending long hours at ECEC centers can have on children's behavioral outcomes (for U.S. evidence see Loeb et al. (2007); for Australian evidence see Bowes, Harrison, Sweller, and Taylor (2009)). Although not Indigenous-specific, the negative behavioral effects of spending longer hours at ECEC centers is less consistent for disadvantaged children. That is, when disadvantaged children attend high-quality settings for long hours, they make gains that are not observed for non-disadvantaged children (Campbell et al., 2012; Loeb et al., 2007).

In the context of Australia's Indigenous children, Leigh and Gong (2009) applied AEDI data to demonstrate that the gap in cognitive skills between Indigenous and non-Indigenous preschool-aged children is largely explained by socioeconomic factors (i.e. about two-thirds of the gap is explained by these factors). Harrison et al. (2010) examined the cognitive and behavioral outcomes of children enrolled in various types of care (e.g. formal and informal care) using the LSAC. The gap between Indigenous and non-Indigenous children in tests of early literacy was found to be larger than the gap between lone parent and two-parent households. Similarly, Indigenous children tended to score more poorly on physical health outcomes than non-Indigenous children, and this difference was much higher than the gap in physical health outcomes between children of English-speaking and children of non-English-speaking backgrounds. Results also point to Indigenous parents having more concerns regarding their children's communication abilities, relative to parents of young non-Indigenous children.

The above studies utilised data that permitted the comparison among various subgroups of mainstream and Australian Indigenous children. The main limitation with respect to these studies was that the outcome measures were designed for non-Indigenous children and, as a consequence, may be inappropriate for measuring the development of Indigenous children. Addressing this concern, Biddle and Arcos Holzinger (2015) used LSIC to explore the links between ECEC participation and the effects on a range of short- and long-term developmental and cognitive outcomes for Indigenous children (Table 6.2).

130 Closing the educational gap

Table 6.2 Cognitive and Non-Cognitive Outcome Measures Used by Biddle and Arcos Holzinger (2015)

Developmental outcomes	Strengths and difficulties Questionnaire total difficulties score Prosocial scale Child is always happy at school
Reading and literacy ability outcomes	Teacher-reported language and literacy Renfrew vocabulary test Progressive Achievement Test in Reading
Abstract reasoning and maths ability outcomes	Teacher-reported maths Progressive Achievement Test in Mathematics Abstract reasoning (Matrix test)

Source: Biddle and Arcos Holzinger (2015)

The authors disaggregate the effects of ECEC by preschool and childcare attendance. In short, results show that while both programs enhance numeracy, reading and behavioral outcomes in the long run, preschool has a stronger impact on short-term cognitive outcomes. Also, in the short run, preschool and childcare attendance have a strong impact only on literacy outcome measures. The Figures below report outcomes at various ages of primary schooling. They compare the outcomes of Indigenous children who had attended preschool and childcare services, relative to those of children who did not attended. Model 1 controls only for ECEC attendance, while model 2 controls for ECEC attendance as well as for a range of other demographic characteristics that could potentially impact the test score analysed. Shaded bars signify statistically significant effects of ECEC participation, and the vertical axis measures the difference in standard deviations. In terms of developmental outcomes, ECEC attendance in model 2 led to a statistically significant decrease in the behavioral difficulties estimated by the SDQ total difficulties test, which points to less developmental difficulties (Figure 6.2).

ECEC attendance also led to improved reading and literacy achievement (Figure 6.3), maths ability and abstract reasoning scores (Figure 6.4), with some differences being statistically significant.

The study also examines the 'dosage' effect of ECEC hours attended. Results reveal that very long hours at childcare are detrimental to the behavioral outcomes of the children. These results provide us with standardised tests that have been assessed for their appropriateness to measuring the development of Indigenous children, which is an advantage over other tests designed for the population of mainstream Australian children.

Although the findings of the above studies do not incorporate children's Indigenous-specific skills and cultural acquisition, they do provide information on how ECEC impacts widely on developmental outcomes. These measures are especially insightful when they have been validated for the population of Indigenous

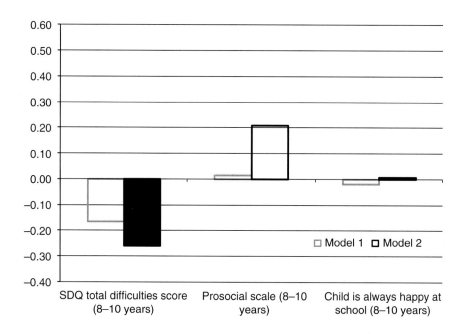

Figure 6.2 The Effect of ECEC Attendance on Behavioural Outcomes
Adapted from Biddle and Arcos Holzinger (2015)

children. Indirect evidence of the importance of ECEC participation on learning outcomes is highlighted by using previous educational experiences as the control variable when analysing the gap between Indigenous and non-Indigenous youth (during adolescence). Differences between the two groups appear to be particularly noticeable with regards to educational expectations, rates of school drop-out and tertiary acceptance rates. At first, these differences appear to be important and significant, however, ranks become non-significant once previous educational experiences are controlled (Biddle & Cameron, 2012). Furthermore, better educational outcomes have been shown to enhance Indigenous-specific measures, as well as to help close the gap in a range of social indicators (Biddle & Cameron, 2012; Dockery, 2010).

The importance of quality ECEC services and staff retention

Ensuring access to ECEC programs for Indigenous families under the Australian federal government's 'Closing the Gap' policies (Department of the Prime Minister and Cabinet, 2016) will not necessarily lead to improved engagement in ECEC or developmental outcomes for children. The real issue is that finding

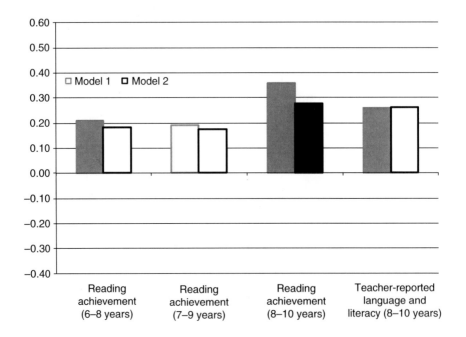

Figure 6.3 The Effect of ECEC on Reading and Literacy Proficiency
Adapted from Biddle and Arcos Holzinger (2015)

quality and affordable ECEC services is still a barrier to urban and regional Indigenous families (Hewitt & Walter, 2014). The gap in ECEC participation by Indigenous status is present in terms of hours attended and age of attendance. Indigenous children tend to attend ECEC services for less time, and begin attendance when they are much older than non-Indigenous children (Lee, 2014). Recent international evidence points to skewed gains from ECEC, with stronger developmental gains made when children have enrolled at ECEC from an earlier age (Kalb, Tabasso, & Zakirova, 2014). Based on this, programs that strive for quality ECEC participation at an early age could go some way to improving the school readiness of Indigenous children.

Although there have been an increasing number of Indigenous-specific programs to incentivise ECEC participation, there are issues with respect to cost and quality of service. McMahon (2015) posits that as these services are not regulated by the NQF there is a possibility that some, while affordable, may not provide a satisfactory level of quality from the parents' perspective. This is problematic given that there is evidence showing that a poor-quality program can be detrimental to a child's development (Daley, McGannon, & Ginnivan, 2012).

Clearly, a gap exists with respect to finding solutions to incentivise the recruitment and retention of competent educators, particularly in remote settings.

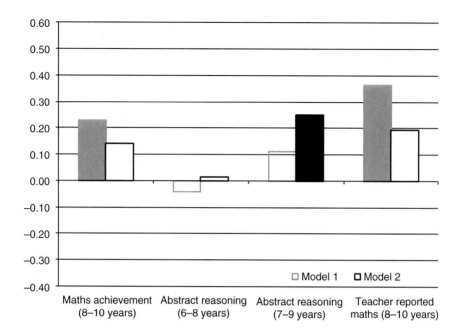

Figure 6.4 The Effect of ECEC on Maths Ability and Abstract Reasoning
Adapted from Biddle and Arcos Holzinger (2015)

Cumming, Sumsion, and Wong (2015) point to widespread problems in retaining adequately trained educators for Indigenous-specific programs. Further, the pressure this creates on educators who remain at the school is that they are often required to take on roles in which they have not been trained. Moreover, programs to train educators in culturally responsive practices are growing internationally, and there is a need to better account for the effects of these training programs on the outcomes of Indigenous children (Preston et al., 2012). This gap is incredibly important given recent evidence showing that higher teacher qualifications are strongly correlated with better student test scores (Warren & Haisken-DeNew, 2013) and the quality of early childhood learning environment (Manning et al., in press).

Partnerships to achieve ECEC policy goals

Targeted ECEC programs, especially those for disadvantaged and minority children, have generally outperformed universal programs (Dumas et al., 2010; Reynolds et al., 2011). This evidence, therefore, suggests that programs specifically targeted to Indigenous families are likely to produce better outcomes and, as a consequence, better engage Indigenous families. Of these programs, National Partnerships to deliver ECEC services for highly disadvantaged Indigenous children (to help meet 'Closing the Gap') show promising results with respect to their effectiveness. Also, the integration of ECEC services has been identified as a way to improve the physical health support provided to vulnerable families and communities, so ECEC services will begin integrating programs aimed at health provision (Department of the Prime Minister and Cabinet, 2016). This is a strategy that could potentially address the health inequalities of Indigenous children, so more program evaluations for these integrated models will be essential to build robust evidence with respect to efficacy.

One example of successful National Partnership programs is the Families as First Teachers (FaFT) program. Operating in the Northern territory for 21 very remote communities, the program is aimed at building family knowledge of ECEC curricula (for example, through parenting workshops, home visits and personal consultations), with the aim of ensuring that Indigenous children in these communities are school-ready. Since the program's inception, the proportion of Indigenous children with developmental vulnerability in the communities serviced has fallen by 5.7 per cent. Surveys from principals where the children were beginning full-time schooling also revealed that the staffs view children who participated in the program to be more ready to actively engage in learning and school activities (Australian Early Development, 2014).

Another promising partnership program is the Home Interaction Program for Parents and Youngsters (HIPPY) (Baker, Piotkowski, & Brooks-Gunn, 1999). HIPPY is a two-year program that aims to train parents and caregivers to teach children important skills at home. The Australian version of the program has an Indigenous focus, but also provides services to disadvantaged non-Indigenous families. An evaluation of five HIPPY Indigenous sites revealed substantial increases in program participation during its second year of operation. Liddell et al. (2011) argue that programs that engage Indigenous families and communities over longer periods of time have higher success rates. Evidence demonstrates that the program worked best in sites where community leaders were involved and where there were strong links between HIPPY staff and other local Indigenous service providers. This compels us to think that implementing integrated service to remote communities is an effective strategy.

While these preliminary results are promising, the research mostly applies qualitative or mixed-methods approaches, which are unable to untangle the effects of the program from other programs, the characteristics of participating families, or changes occurring through time. Hence, these programs would benefit from conducting rigorous quantitative evaluations that account for these potential confounding factors.

So where to now?

Are we now placed to successfully answer the questions we posed in the introduction? That is: (1) How can we close the educational gap between Indigenous and non-Indigenous children in a meaningful and sustainable way? (2) Can education break the vicious cycle that Indigenous people face in rural and remote communities?

With regard to the first question, the policy impetus to 'Closing the Gap' in the ECEC access for Indigenous children has generated a range of Indigenous-specific programs aimed to improve the educational attainment and development of Indigenous children. This policy focus on ECEC has generated a wave of recent research specifically aimed at assessing the impact of ECEC programs on Indigenous children. These recent studies have an advantage over earlier studies as they account for factors that are unique to the Indigenous population. Recent analyses that utilise development measures validated for Indigenous children point to the important cognitive and developmental gains that can be made for Indigenous children by engaging them in quality ECEC programs.

There is, however, an important gap with regard to the impact of ECEC on Indigenous-specific and subjective wellbeing measures, which are of vital importance to Indigenous communities (Dockery, 2010). Moreover, while the policy focus has been on providing access to ECEC services, analysis on the determinants of ECEC participation shows that access and affordability of ECEC services are not always the main concerns of parents choosing to participate or not to participate in ECEC programs. Indigenous parents place an important weight on ECEC providing a culturally responsive environment, especially by employing staff that understand and embrace Indigenous values and culture. A related concern, particularly that of parents and caregivers, is the quality provision of ECEC services. While the implementation of the National Quality Framework (NQF) improved the quality of ECEC programs nationally, there is still high variability of ECEC quality across areas by socio-economic disadvantage as well as a lack of detailed evidence explaining how area-level disadvantage affects the ECEC experience of Indigenous children (Breunig, Gong, & Trott, 2014; Warner & Gradus, 2011). There is also little quantitative research exploring the importance of ECEC quality on the decision of Indigenous parents to participate in ECEC programs. Similarly, there is a lack of evidence on the effect of varying levels of quality on the cognitive and developmental outcomes of Indigenous children that participate in ECEC. Finally, while there is preliminary evidence pointing to the effectiveness of focused ECEC programs aimed at highly disadvantaged Indigenous communities, these results, for the most part, do not implement a rigorous framework to control for other confounding factors. This alone limits our knowledge on the extent to which these programs are economically efficient (i.e. cost-effective) and better enhance the outcomes of Indigenous children relative to standard approaches of ECEC delivery.

In terms of answering the second question, the evidence is still inconclusive. Can education break the vicious cycle that Indigenous people face in rural and remote communities? We should really be asking, 'Can the programs and methods of implementation, engagement and evaluation that we use break the vicious cycle in the long-term'? Until we conduct rigorous empirical evaluations, particularly randomised control trials that follow individuals over the life course, it will be difficult to fully answer this question with any degree of confidence. Although

136 Closing the educational gap

there are empirical studies that focus on the problems discussed throughout this chapter, much of the literature is no more than correlational in nature. This is not to say that the majority of studies are poor in quality. Rather, the point is that we can do a lot better.

What is required are longitudinal studies that provide alternative explanations that are both parsimonious and causally explicit – such studies may call into question the validity of a range of assumptions that underpin much theorizing in this area. We argue that researchers in this area more readily embrace parsimony and support the incremental development of theoretical complexity; but only where tractability, testability, and as a result, utility are not compromised.

A special thanks

The authors would like to acknowledge the assistance provided by Dr Nicholas Biddle and Ms Lilia Arcos Holzinger in the development and feedback of this chapter. Their combined experience and knowledge in this area were incredibly useful in developing a thorough review of the salient literature.

Note

1 "The National Quality Framework (NQF) is the result of an agreement between all Australian governments to work together to provide better educational and developmental outcomes for children using education and care services. The NQF introduces a new quality standard to improve education and care across long day care, family day care, preschool/kindergarten, and outside school hours care" (Australian Children's Education & Care Quality Authority, 2015).

Reference List

Australian Bureau of Statistics. (2015). *Aboriginal and torres strait islander skills: Education, learning and skills.*

Australian Children's Education & Care Quality Authority. (2015). *Introducing the national quality framework.*

Australian Early Development Census. (2014). *Community story: Families as first teachers.* Northern Territory.

Australian Government. (2016). *Overview of footprints in time – The Longitudinal Study of Indigenous Children (LSIC).*

Baker, A.J.L., Piotkowski, C.S., & Brooks-Gunn, J. (1999). The home instruction program for preschool youngsters (HIPPY). *The Future of Children, 9*(1), 116–133.

Barnett, W.S. (1998). Long-term cognitive and academic effects of early childhood education on children in poverty. *Preventive Medicine, 27*(2), 204–207. Retrieved from http://www.sciencedirect.com/science/article/pii/S0091743598902754.

Baxter, J., & Hand, K. (2013). *Access to early childhood education in Australia.* Melbourne, Australia: Australian Institute of Family Studies.

Biddle, N. (2007). Indigenous Australians and preschool education: Who is attending? *Australian Journal of Early Childhood, 32*(3), 9. Retrieved from http://search.

informit.com.au/fullText;res=IELAPA;dn=200710368; http://search.informit.com. au/payPerView;dn=200710368;res=IELAPA;type=pdf; http://search.informit.com. au/documentSummary;dn=200710368;res=IELAPA.

Biddle, N. (2012). *CAEPR Indigenous population project 2011 census papers: Population and age structure*. Canberra, Australia: Centre for Aboriginal Economic Policy Research.

Biddle, N., & Arcos Holzinger, L. (2015). *The relationship between early childhood education and care (ECEC) and the outcomes of Indigenous children: Evidence from the Longitudinal Study of Indigenous Children (LSIC)* (103/2015). Canberra, Australia: Centre for Aboriginal Economic Policy Research (CAEPR).

Biddle, N., & Cameron, T. (2012). *Potential factors influencing indigenous education participation and achievement: Research report*. Adelaide: NCVER.

Bishop, A.R., Berryman, M.A., Wearmouth, J.B., & Peter, M. (2012). Developing an effective education reform model for indigenous and other minoritized students. *School Effectiveness and School Improvement, 23*(1), 49–70. doi:10.1080/0924345 3.2011.647921.

Boocock, S.S. (1995). Early childhood programs in other nations: goals and outcomes. *The Future of Children, 5*(3), 94–114. Retrieved from http://www.jstor. org/stable/1602369.

Bowes, J., Harrison, L., Sweller, N., & Taylor, A. (2009). *From child care to school: Influences on children's adjustment and achievement in the year before school and the first year of school*. Children and Families Research Centre, Macquarie University and School of Teacher Education, Charles Sturt University.

Brennan, D., & Adamson, E. (2014). *Financing the future: An equitable and sustainable approach to early childhood education and care* (01/14). Social Policy Research Centre, University of New South Wales.

Breunig, R.V., Gong, X., & Trott, D. (2014). The new national quality framework: Quantifying some of the effects on labour supply, child care demand and household finances for two-parent households. *Economic Record, 90*(288), 1–16. Retrieved from http://onlinelibrary.wiley.com/doi/10.1111/1475–4932.12059/full.

Camilli, G., Vargas, S., Ryan, S., & Barnett, W.S. (2010). Meta-analysis of the effects of early education interventions on cognitive and social development. *Teachers College Record, 112*(3), 579–620. Retrieved from http://www.tcrecord. org/DefaultFiles/SendFileToPublic.asp?ft=pdf&FilePath=c:%5CWebSites%5C www_tcrecord_org_documents%5C38_15440.pdf&fid=38_15440&aid=2&RID =15440&pf=Content.asp?ContentID=15440; https://www.tcrecord.org/Signin. asp?cc=1&r=2

Campbell, F., Pungello, E., Burchinal, M., Kainz, K., Pan, Y., Wasik, B., . . . Ramey, C.T. (2012). Adult outcomes as a function of an early childhood educational program: An Abecedarian Project follow-up. *Developmental Psychology, 48*(4), 1033.

Colbung, M., Glover, A., Rau, C., & Ritchie, J. (2007). *Indigenous peoples and perspectives in early childhood education theorising early childhood practice: Emerging dialogues*. Castle Hill, NSW: Pademelon Press.

Council of Australian Governments. (2012). *Steering committee for the review of government service provision (SCROGSP) – Triennial report*. Canberra, Australia.

Cumming, T., Sums ion, J., & Wong, S. (2015). Rethinking early childhood workforce sustainability in the context of Australia's early childhood education and care reforms. *International Journal of Child Care and Education Policy, 9*(1), 1–15. Retrieved from http://link.springer.com/article/10.1007/s40723-015-0005-z.

Daley, J., McGannon, C., & Ginnivan, L. (2012). *Game-changers: Economic reform priorities for Australia.* Sydney: Grattan Institute.

De Maio, J.A., Zubrick, S.R., Silburn, S.R., Lawrence, D.M., Mitrou, F.G., Dalby, R.B., . . . Cox, A. (2005). *The western Australian aboriginal child health survey: Measuring the social and emotional wellbeing of Aboriginal children and intergenerational effects of forced separation.* The Western Australian Aboriginal Child Health Survey.

Department of Prime Minister and Cabinet. (2016). *Closing the gap.* Canberra, Australia: Commonwealth of Australia.

Dockery, A.M. (2010). Culture and wellbeing: The case of indigenous Australians. *Social Indicators Research, 99*(2), 315–332. doi:10.1007/s11205-010-9582-y.

Dockery, A.M. (2011). *Traditional culture and the wellbeing of indigenous Australians: An analysis of the 2008 NATSISS.* Centre for Labour Market Research, Curtin University.

Dockett, S., Perry, B., & Kearney, E. (2010). *School readiness: What does it mean for indigenous children, families, schools and communities?* Canberra, Australia & Melbourne: Australian Institute of Health and Welfare & Australian Institute of Family Studies.

Dumas, C., Lefranc, A., et al. (2010). *Early schooling and later outcomes: Evidence from pre-school extension in France.* THEMA (Théorie Economique, Modélisation et Applications), Université de Cergy-Pontoise.

Gilley, T., Tayler, C., Niklas, F., & Cloney, D. (2015). Too late and not enough for some children: early childhood education and care (ECEC) program usage patterns in the years before school in Australia. *International Journal of Child Care and Education Policy, 9*(1), 1–15. doi:10.1186/s40723-015-0012-0.

Goldfeld, S., O'Connor, E., O'Connor, M., Sayers, M., Moore, T., Kvalsvig, A., & Brinkman, S. (2015). The role of preschool in promoting children's healthy development: Evidence from an Australian population cohort. *Early Childhood Research Quarterly, 35*(1), 40–48.

Grace, R., Bowes, J., & Elcombe, E. (2014). Child participation and family engagement with early childhood education and care services in disadvantaged Australian communities. *International Journal of Early Childhood, 46*(2), 271–298. Retrieved from http://link.springer.com/article/10.1007/s13158-014-0112-y; https://www.infona.pl/resource/bwmeta1.element.springer-a9618902-3945-346c-b731-bc70b37ec995.

Harrison, L.J., Goldfeld, S., Metcalfe, E., & Moore, T. (2012). *Early learning programs that promote children's developmental and educational outcomes.* Closing the Gap Clearinghouse.

Harrison, L.J., Ungerer, J., Smith, G., Zubrick, S., Wise, S., Press, F., . . . The, L.R.C. (2010). *Child care and early education in Australia – the longitudinal study of Australian Children* (40). Canberra, Australia.

Heckman, J.J. (2006). Skill formation and the economics of investing in disadvantaged children. *Science, 312*(5782), 1900–1902.

Hewitt, B., & Walter, M. (2014). Preschool participation among indigenous children in Australia. *Family Matters, 95,* 41. Retrieved from http://search.informit.com.au/documentSummary;dn=837543241225036;res=IELFSC.

Kalb, G., Tabasso, D., & Zakirova, R. (2014). *Children's participation in early childhood education and care, and their developmental outcomes by year 5: A comparison between disadvantaged and advantaged children.* Melbourne Institute of Applied Economic and Social Research.

Lee, K. (2014). Impact of child care arrangements on Australian children's cognitive outcome: Moderation effects of parental factors. *Child & Family Social Work,* 21(2), 1–12. doi:10.1111/cfs.12127.

Leigh, A., & Gong, X. (2009). Estimating cognitive gaps between indigenous and non-indigenous Australians. *Education Economics, 17*(2), 239–261. Retrieved from http://www.tandfonline.com/doi/abs/10.1080/09645290802069418.

Liddell, M., Barnett, T., Diallo Roost, F., & McEachran, J. (2011). *Investing in our future: An evaluation of the national rollout of the Home Interaction Program for Parents and Youngsters (HIPPY): Final report to the Department of Education, Employment and Workplace Relations.* Victoria: HIPPY Australia, Brotherhood of St. Laurence.

Loeb, S., Bridges, M., Bassok, D., Fuller, B., & Rumberger, R.W. (2007). How much is too much? The influence of preschool centers on children's social and cognitive development. *Economics of Education Review, 26*(1), 52–66. doi:10.1016/j.econedurev.2005.11.005.

Manning, M. (2008). *Economic evaluation of the effects of early childhood intervention programs on adolescent outcomes.* (PhD), Griffith University, Brisbane.

Manning, M. (2014). Developmental interventions on children and familial wellbeing. In S. Garvis & D. Pendergast (Eds.), *Health and wellbeing in the early years* (pp. 176–187). Cambridge: Cambridge University Press.

Manning, M., Garvis, S., Fleming, C., & Wong, G. (in press). *The relationship between teacher qualification and the quality of the early childhood and learning environment: A systematic review*: Campbell Collaboration Library of Systematic Reviews.

Manning, M., Homel, R., & Smith, C. (2010). A meta-analysis of the effects of early developmental prevention programs in at-risk populations on non-health outcomes in adolescence. *Children and Youth Services Review, 32*(4), 506–519.

McKenzie, F., & Da Costa, R. (2015). *Early childhood development in Australia: Challenging the system* (2). La Trobe University.

McMahon, S. (2015). Literature review: What can we learn from the childcare and early education literature? *Children Australia, 40*(01), 87–90. Retrieved from http://journals.cambridge.org/abstract_S1035077214000480; http://journals.cambridge.org/action/displayAbstract?fromPage=online&aid=9641189&fileI d=S1035077214000480.

McTurk, N., Lea, T., Robinson, G., Nutton, G., & Carapetis, J.R. (2011). Defining and assessing the school readiness of indigenous Australian children. *Australasian Journal of Early Childhood, 36*(1), 69. Retrieved from http://search.informit.com.au/documentSummary;dn=950524743942916;res=IELHSS.

Miller, M. (2004). *Ensuring the rights of indigenous children.* Washington, DC: UNICEF Innocenti Research Centre.

Moss, B., Harper, H., Silburn, S., et al. (2015). Strengthening aboriginal child development in central Australia through a universal preschool readiness program. *Australasian Journal of Early Childhood, 40*(4), 13. Retrieved from https://search.informit.com.au/documentSummary;dn=840481564493697;res=IELHSS.

Nores, M., Belfield, C.R., Barnett, W.S., & Schweinhart, L. (2005). Updating the economic impacts of the High/Scope Perry Preschool program. *Educational Evaluation and Policy Analysis, 27*(3), 245–261. Retrieved from http://epa.sagepub.com/content/27/3/245.short.

140 Closing the educational gap

Nutton, G.D. (2013). *The effectiveness of mobile preschool (Northern Territory) in improving school readiness for very remote indigenous children.* Charles Darwin University. Retrieved from http://espace.cdu.edu.au/view/cdu:39050 Available from espace.cdu.edu.au.

Nutton, G.D., Bell, J., Fraser, J., Elliott, A., Andrews, R., Louden, W., & Carapetis, J. (2011). *Extreme preschool: Mobile preschool in Australia's northern territory.* In 24th international congress for school effectiveness and improvement.

O'Conner, M., Fox, S., Hinz, B., & Cole, H. (2016). *Quality early education for all: Fostering, entrepreneurial, resilient and capable leaders* (01/2016). Melbourne: Mitchell Institute.

Preston, J.P., Cottrell, M., Pelletier, T.R., & Pearce, J.V. (2012). Aboriginal early childhood education in Canada: Issues of context. *Journal of Early Childhood Research, 10*(1), 3–18. Retrieved from http://ecr.sagepub.com/content/10/1/3.short.

Productivity Commission. (2011). *Early childhood development workforce research report.* Melbourne: Productivity Commission.

Productivity Commission. (2014). Childcare and early childhood learning inquiry report No. 73. Canberra, Australia: Productivity Commission

Productivity Commission. (2016). *Report on government services: Early childhood education and care.* Australian Government.

Purdie, N., Reid, K., Frigo, T., Stone, A., & Kleinhenz, E. (2011). *Literacy and numeracy learning: Lessons from the longitudinal literacy and numeracy study for indigenous students* (7–2011). Sydney: Australian Council for Educational Research.

Reyes-García, V., Kightley, E., Ruiz-Mallén, I., Fuentes-Peláez, N., Demps, K., Huanca, T., & Martínez-Rodríguez, M.R. (2010). Schooling and local environmental knowledge: Do they complement or substitute each other? *International Journal of Educational Development, 30*(3), 305–313. Retrieved from http://www.sciencedirect.com/science/article/pii/S0738059309001503.

Reynolds, A., Temple, J., Ou, S., Arteaga, I., & White, B. (2011). School-based early childhood education and age-28 well-being: Effects by timing, dosage, and subgroups. *Science, 333*(6040), 360–364.

Savage, C., Hindle, R., Meyer, L.H., Hynds, A., Penetito, W., & Sleeter, C.E. (2011). Culturally responsive pedagogies in the classroom: Indigenous student experiences across the curriculum. *Asia-Pacific Journal of Teacher Education, 39*(3), 183–198. Retrieved from http://www.tandfonline.com/doi/abs/10.108 0/1359866X.2011.588311; http://www.tandfonline.com/doi/full/10.1080/1359866X.2011.588311.

Trudgett, M., & Grace, R. (2011). Engaging with early childhood education and care services: The perspectives of Indigenous Australian mothers and their young children. *Kulumun, 1* (pp. 15–37). Retrieved from http://www.researchonline.mq.edu.au/vital/access/services/Download/mq:19168/DS01.

Warner, M.E., & Gradus, R.H.J.M. (2011). The consequences of implementing a child care voucher scheme: Evidence from Australia, the Netherlands and the USA. *Social Policy & Administration, 45*(5), 569–592. doi:10.1111/j.1467–9515.2011.00787.x.

Warren, D., & Haisken-DeNew, J.P. (2013). *Early bird catches the worm: The causal impact of pre-school participation and teacher qualifications on year 3 National NAPLAN Cognitive Tests* (34/13). Melbourne Institute of Applied Economic and Social Research, The University of Melbourne.

Chapter 7

Where to next for early childhood education and care? The importance of an interdisciplinary approach

The final chapter of the book provides suggestions for what is needed as the next step in the progression of Australian early childhood education and care. Moving beyond individual disciplines that have been explored, the final chapter proposes that an interdisciplinary approach is needed to provide a better foundation for early childhood. An interdisciplinary approach allows the different disciplines to work together, strengthening the overall impact and providing a shared approach to working with children and their families. The chapter concludes with a list of key considerations for the future of Australian early childhood education and care. Suggestions are made to different stakeholders within different disciplines. It is hoped that by developing a better understanding of the Australian early childhood education and care landscape, future change can be progressive and provide support for all Australian children and their families.

Interdisciplinary ways of working provides opportunities for significant improvement in Australian early childhood education and care. Within Australia, many disciplines involved in early childhood education and care work in isolation, often unaware of the child and family in different contexts. For example, a child may have a visit to a maternal and child health nurse for a health check. The assessment may draw upon learning activities the child may be familiar with, such as naming colours. The nurse will conduct the assessment in isolation with the child and family; however, some of the information may have been able to be supplied by an educator. Likewise, the findings of the health check are not shared with the educator, meaning the educator is not provided with all information regarding the child's learning and development to plan adequate learning experiences for the child in an early childhood setting. Another scenario could be that the child may not choose to label colours for the nurse, even though the educator has seen the child do this many times. The nurse would then assess the child as not competent for that particular assessment item. Imagine what could be achieved in this example if the nurse and the educator worked together. The possibilities for supporting the child and family are endless.

Interdisciplinary ways of working allows the sharing of information, skills and knowledge. A working team brings together their strengths from their own discipline and is able to complement the other disciplines – for example, combining an economics perspective with an education perspective. Interdisciplinary ways of working are considered a possible future for early childhood education and care. This chapter will explore some of the literature regarding interdisciplinary teams before providing two examples of projects from Australia. The next part of the chapter will focus on providing considerations for the future for Australian early childhood education and care. These are directed towards stakeholders to prompt further discussion and hopefully action around improvements for early childhood education and care. The considerations are also relevant for the international context. While this book has focused specifically on the Australian context, lessons can be learnt for early childhood education and care across the world.

Interdisciplinary ways of working

Establishing interdisciplinary teams involves negotiating roles and spaces as the traditional work boundaries are crossed (Waitoller & Kozleski, 2013). Boundaries indicate a disjuncture in practice between sites that have relevance to each other. Boundary practices are those practices in which the involved players are engaged (Waitoller & Kozleski, 2013). Therefore, the development of neophyte professionals, management of the complex health issues of patients, or the support of children's learning can lead to boundary practices as common goals are pursued in different ways by different groups of players, depending upon the perspective held.

Williams (2014) concluded in her study on teacher educators that managing different perspectives necessitated building "trusting and respectful relationships through dialogue" (p. 325). However, obstacles to working inter-professionally include: communication; building networks (Brener et al., 2007); and other cultural variations between professional groups (Clarke, Jones, & Armstrong, 2007).

From a lifecourse or developmental perspective, childhood wellbeing is typically associated with developmental transitions between different stages in life. Ben-Arieh (2006, p. 2) states: "Often, especially among young children, the standards for development are based on a preferred adolescent or adult outcome, implying the need to prepare children for their transition into later stages in life or to monitor the developmental process". Moreover, Manning (2014) argues that the isolated efforts of individuals, including individual disciplines, cannot solve all problems or significantly improve the outcomes of children in a disciplinary vacuum. Rather, a holistic, inter-professional approach is required; this involves a major paradigm shift beyond the current system of silos.

While the academic literature can guide inter-professional education in health care settings, there continues to be limited information to help guide a similar process in relation to educational settings (Salm et al., 2010; Tourse et al., 2005), especially the early childhood sector (Anderson, 2013). This suggests a real need in research to explore relationships between health and education professionals as a shift forward to enhance children's outcomes.

Some of the challenges to inter-professional training have come from: a tradition of educating professionals by immersing them into one chosen profession, the proliferation of "silo" models within curricula, and a structure created by discipline-specific professional codes and credentialing/licensing bodies that often further constrain collaborative efforts (Bluteau & Jackson, 2009). There is also the perception that opportunity for interdisciplinary collaboration in educational settings is limited due to time constraints (Bronstein & Abramson, 2003; Friend & Cook, 2010).

Another limitation has been the marginalization of early childhood education pedagogical practice. Cheeseman (2007) warns that the interdisciplinary teams can sometimes marginalize early childhood educators because of their pedagogical practice. In relationships, she suggests early childhood educators may feel less respected as they do not come from a health background. Medical staff may also look down upon early childhood educators. In another study, Cumming and Wong (2012) also noted the differences between the professions working together. In their study, they noted an unequal relationship with health professionals, with perceptions of professional bias that valued the knowledge of medical staff over the knowledge of educators. Cumming and Wong (2012) concluded that the status of educators was low compared to health professionals.

Despite the evidence suggesting the importance of interdisciplinary teamwork in early childhood education, few Australian studies have been able to show the practices of working together within Australia (Wong, Sumison, & Press, 2012). What is needed are more examples within the field of productive relationships of education and health professionals working together. This has been acknowledged by some researchers and the Australian government with some studies starting to be supported. A snapshot of some of these studies is provided below.

Interdisciplinary education in the early years

A recent 2014 Australian project was funded by the Australian Government Office for Learning and Teaching entitled "Interdisciplinary Education for the Early Years". The project is a consortium of Flinders University, Charles Sturt University, Gowrie South Australia, Queensland University of Technology, University of South Australia and the University of Western Australia. The project is still under way.

The outcome of the project is to develop a statement of common outcomes for children from birth to five years of age that recognizes various disciplinary foci. The goal is to develop a national interdisciplinary learning and teaching framework to inform curriculum for the education of professionals across diverse disciplines who work with children aged birth to five years and their families. The development of a national interdisciplinary learning and teaching framework will promote professional collaboration and inter-professional alignment. It will enable professionals who work with children in the early years to collaboratively

144 Where to next for early childhood education

challenge and co-create shared perspectives on all aspects of the early years, including child protection.

St Kilda kindergarten and maternal child nurse project

This study reported the findings of two professionals, an educator and the outreach maternal child health nurse, working together in a long day care centre to address the need for a more comprehensive check prior to school entry (Garvis et al., 2015). Over a period of five years, these professionals have collaborated together to work with families to improve children's outcomes and developed their own health check. The number of health checks improved in the preschool and the educator was also able to implement planning for children based on their assessment. The educator and the nurse were also able to have detailed conversations about issues that arose regarding children and their families. This type of collaboration allowed the teams to employ a diverse skill set and to respond to children's different requirements and needs as well as those of families. However, within Australia, there are many obstacles to working in an inter-professional collaboration, including communication, differences in conceptualising needs and cultural variations between professional groups. The study recognised that such a model between an educator and a maternal child health nurse may not be possible because of different expectations and ways of working. However this small study does show the glimpses of what is possible within Australia when different disciplines do work together to enhance and support young children and their families.

What can be seen from both of these studies are the possibilities for enhancements in the lives of young children and their families. By having common terminology, greater collaboration and ways of working can be achieved, as topics are understood by all disciplines involved. In the second example, the strong interdisciplinary partnership provided enhanced professional practice and improvements for children and their families. It provides professionals an example of what can be achieved when two professionals work together in an early childhood setting. More examples of ways of working within interdisciplinary teams are needed to provide professionals with evidence of what can be achieved as well as the different strategies and approaches that may be needed.

'Communities that care' and 'pathways to prevention' projects

Communities That Care (CTC) (Arthur et al., 2010) and the Pathways to Prevention Program (Homel et al., 2006) have provided some valuable lessons for the development and implementation of future developmental prevention initiatives. These two programs provide an example of how education, policy, health and developmental lifecourse perspectives can work together. One of the key lessons is that the isolated efforts of individual institutions (e.g. schools) cannot solve problems caused by system failures. Moreover, the inequities in wellbeing between mainstream and marginalised communities, exacerbated by the growing concentration of multiple disadvantaged families living in low socio-economic-status areas, pose significant challenges to policy development and cannot be overcome without a major paradigm shift.

Underpinned by ecological and developmental systems theory and a fairly broad range of empirical analyses, developmental prevention offers a number of benefits for disadvantaged and vulnerable children that persist into late adolescence and early adulthood (Manning, Homel, & Smith, 2010). Despite this, few interventions have been implemented by the social and education sectors on a large scale. Moreover, the interventions tend to lack important collaborative relationships with key institutions within communities.

A problem that faces policy makers is that systems embedded in communities (e.g. education systems and the individual schools within that system) are not 'system-ready', or for that matter 'evidence-ready' (Little & Maughan, 2010). More concerning is that the social and education sectors face concentrated disadvantage and remain largely locked into a model of isolated impact, focused on the independent activities of individual organizations. What is required, however, is a model of collective impact. Collective impact initiatives are described by Kania and Kramer (2011) as:

> . . . long-term commitments by a group of important actors from different sectors to a common agenda for solving a specific social problem. Their actions are supported by a shared measurement system, mutually reinforcing activities, and ongoing communications, and are staffed by an independent backbone organization
>
> (p. 39).

In light of the obvious challenges that policy makers face, two fundamental goals exist: (1) to build a set of structured processes and resources that strengthen the developmental system in socially disadvantaged communities to make possible sustainable improvements in the wellbeing of children; and (2) to test the processes: (a) for efficacy in fostering community coalitions empowered to achieve collective impact, and (b) for transportability to new communities.

Critically, a central objective is to make such an advance possible in disadvantaged or vulnerable areas. This requires the development of a national infrastructure that attempts to move away from the funding of individual services in isolation to a more coordinated approach. This scenario would require diverse organizations to come together as clearly focused, well-resourced, skilled and fully collaborative partnerships to solve a small number of specific problems that they have identified as priorities on the basis of local data. These collaborative partnerships, or community coalitions, would empower schools (and the teachers in those schools) and community agencies to transcend system silos; foster ethical practice and respectful relationships; and deliver goal-directed, quantitatively evaluated, evidence-based resources that promote child wellbeing.

146 Where to next for early childhood education

One of the best contemporary examples of such a system is Communities That Care (CTC) (Feinberg et al., 2010; Kania & Kramer, 2011). CTC creates community coalitions that follow an evidence-based process to coordinate the assessment, planning and implementation of evidence-based programs that enhance quality of life by minimising risks and providing opportunities for change. As successful as this program has been, CTC still struggles to succeed in socially disadvantaged communities where mobilising residents and local organizations is difficult and commitment to evidence-based programs is less strong (Brown, Feinberg, & Greenberg, 2010). Evidence from CTC underlines the critical importance of providing technical assistance for both prevention delivery systems and for the evidence-based programs that they are supposed to deliver.

To transcend system silos, policy makers should aim to: (1) increase the efficacy of individual child-serving organizations (e.g. schools) to operate as part of a wide and integrated system; (2) enhance the capacity of people at every level of an organisation (e.g. teachers) to review and understand their role as part of the overarching developmental system; (3) facilitate openness and commitment to change and organisational reform where needed; (4) motivate clear-headed reflection on the appropriateness of current practice and reduce the use of ineffective and inefficient strategies; and (5) translate knowledge about the causes of poor developmental outcomes into well-implemented evidence-based developmental prevention programs.

Considerations for the future

To provide future direction for early childhood education within Australia, we believe it is important to summarise the main considerations for each group of stakeholders. It is hoped that by raising attention around these areas, further discussion can lead to change – in particular, a focus on different disciplines working together.

Suggestions for policy development

- Commitment is necessary for the universal access agreement for all children to have access to early childhood services. This agreement should not be dependent on the political cycle or funding. While all children have access to education at five years of age, the same provision should be made for children in the year before schooling.
- Early childhood education and care policy should be permanently housed within the Education portfolio of governments. This provides early childhood with equal status to primary education, and allows for smoother transition of programs and policies between early childhood education and primary education.
- Parental leave requires greater government attention and support within Australia. While most developed countries have extended parental leave

based on research regarding children's health and development, Australia does not appear as committed to the youngest of children and their families. Adequate maternity and paternity leave can also provide greater equality for women and men within a society.

- Australian families deserve to have access to high-quality early childhood services that are easy to access and affordable. Other developed countries have been able to achieve quality, accessibility and affordability for families. It is hoped the Australian government can see the long-term economic benefits of adequately funding early childhood and is again able to draw upon findings from other countries. Such adequate programs also reduce child poverty in a country by allowing families to work while their children are provided with early childhood education.

- A long-term plan for early childhood education and care (including early intervention) is needed that extends beyond the immediate three-year political cycle. The long-term plan requires commitment from all parties to ensure adequate funding and support over the next 20 years for all Australians. This would provide adequate funding and support for early childhood and early intervention, providing strong recognition of its importance within the lives of young children and their families. A long-term commitment could also become a building block for future societal change and provide a number of societal, economic, education and health benefits.

Suggestions for university training

- Early childhood teacher education needs to provide adequate coverage of all age ranges within early childhood, including infants and toddlers. This also extends to adequate professional experience days with all age groups.

- All professions that work directly with children and their families need to understand the roles of other professionals. Interdisciplinary ways of working should be considered as important within all learning programs at university.

- All professions also require training in culturally sensitive practices to provide better ways of working with children and their families.

- The government needs to give continued support to ACECQA in reviewing early childhood teacher education programs across Australia. The organisation is able to monitor and assess the learning that is taking place, as well as provide a list of accredited providers. This leads to a standard of qualification within the early childhood profession and allows for a benchmark for early childhood teacher education.

Suggestions for professionalization

- To allow the early childhood profession to understand all of the changes and for changes to be implemented effectively, time scales need to be considered. According to the Education Change model (Chapter 3), change can take up

148 Where to next for early childhood education

to 10 years for complete implementation. During this time the professions need to be provided with strong leadership and professional learning experiences. This means that adequate opportunities need to be provided for professional learning, as well as allowing the profession opportunities to up-skill with leadership within the field.

- A better commitment is needed to incentivise the recruitment and retention of competent professionals to remote settings, especially educators.

Suggestions for research

- In Australia there is a lack of research on actual practices of interdisciplinary practice within early childhood. More research that leads to information about productive partnerships and ways of working is needed. This includes medical and educational professionals working together with young children and their families, as well as economists and criminologists.
- There is limited longitudinal research within Australia that tracks the benefits of participation in early childhood education settings. There is especially a gap with literature related to the impact of early childhood education and care on Indigenous-specific and subjective wellbeing measures, which are important to Indigenous Australian communities. More research is needed that provides societal and economic benefits for policy makers, especially return on investment and cost-benefit modeling. This could also be extended to other government policies aligned with early childhood education settings, including paid parental leave.
- Research is also needed on how to better communicate findings to policy makers to ensure they are able to make informed decisions based on evidence.

Interdisciplinary ways of working within the international context

Interdisciplinary ways of working provides new possibilities not only for Australia, but the larger international early childhood context. By understanding how the different disciplines operate, a shared understanding can be developed to help improve and enhance early childhood education and care in all countries. As yet, few countries have moved beyond disciplines to having professionals and policy makers work together. The considerations listed above may then also be relevant to an international context interested in improving quality, affordability and access. In particular, the Education Change Model, in which policy changes can take up to 10 years for implementation, is worthy of consideration. This means that all professionals, governments and policy makers must be interested in long-term investment to support long-term growth in quality.

Research within the international context is also needed about interdisciplinary ways of working, especially longitudinal studies. Such research would allow for cross-fertilization of findings and ideas, leading to new understandings and practices within policy and practice. Comparative international research would be highly important for benchmarking around quality and provision.

Finally, in many countries early childhood education and care is at a crossroad. While universal access, learning programs, mandatory teacher qualifications and family assistance have been implemented, new ways of understanding are needed to provide improvement within the early childhood sector. Interdisciplinary ways of working provide a new frontier for early childhood education and care, allowing policy makers and professionals to improve and enhance quality further. Commitment to interdisciplinary ways of working, however, is needed.

Conclusion

Australian early childhood has a diverse landscape. Over the years it has been subject to numerous changes and developments. It is hoped that by looking at this book from a number of different perspectives, a new understanding can be developed about ways forward to support young children and their families. It is hoped that readers of this book have a stronger understanding of the past and current contexts and are able to make informed decisions about the future for Australian early childhood education and care. It is hoped that by exploring new ways of working, such as in interdisciplinary teams, better outcomes can be achieved for children, their families and the wider society. A stronger commitment to Australian children and their families is needed and requires decisions that are based on evidence. Other developed countries around the world have had success with early childhood policy, which has led to a number of changes in regards to reduction in poverty, equality between the sexes and enhanced child outcomes. It is time for Australia to also make such a commitment and undertake a long-term plan for the future. All Australian children and families deserve strong support and commitment, starting with high-quality early childhood. Now is the time for change.

References

Anderson, E.M. (2013). Preparing the next generation of early childhood teachers: The emerging role of interprofessional education and collaboration in teacher education. *Journal of Early Childhood Teacher Education, 34*(1), 22–35.

Arthur, M., Hawkins, J., Brown, E., Briney, J., Oesterle, S., & Abbott, R. (2010). Implementation of the communities that care prevention system by coalitions in the community youth development study. *Journal of Community Psychology, 38*(2), 245–258.

Ben-Arieh, A. (2006). *Measuring and monitoring the well-being of young children around the world.* Background paper prepares for the Education for All Global Monitoring Report 2007, UNESCO. Retrieved from http://unesdoc.unesco.org/images/0014/001474/147444e.pdf.

Bluteau, P., & Jackson, A. (2009). *Inter-professional education: Making it happen.* New York: Palgrave Macmillan.

150 Where to next for early childhood education

Brener, N., Wheeler, L., Wolfe, L., Vernon-Smiley, M., & Caldart-Olsen, L. (2007). Health services: Results from the school health policies and programs study. *The Journal of School Health, 77*(8), 464–485.

Bronstein, L.R., & Abramson, J.S. (2003). Understanding socialization of teachers and social workers: Groundwork for collaboration in the schools. *Families in Society, 84*(3), 323–330.

Brown, L., Feinberg, M., & Greenberg, M. (2010). Determinants of community coalition ability to support evidence-based programs. *Prevention Science, 11*(3), 287–297.

Clark, T.D., Jones, M.C., & Armstrong, C.P. (2007). The dynamic structure of management support systems: Theory development, research focus, and direction, *MIS Quarterly, 31*(3), 579–615.

Cheeseman, S. (2007). Pedagogical silences in Australian early childhood social policy. *Contemporary Issues in Early Childhood, 8,* 244–254.

Cumming, T., & Wong, S. (2012). Professionals don't play: Challenges for early childhood educators working in a transdisciplinary early intervention team. *Australasian Journal of Early Childhood, 37*(1), 127–135.

Feinberg, M., Jones, D., Greenberg, M., Osgood, D., & Bontempo, D. (2010). Effects of the communities that care model in Pennsylvania on change in adolescent risk and problem behaviors. *Prevention Science, 11*(2), 163–171.

Friend, M., & Cook, L. (2010). *Interactions: Collaboration skills for school professionals.* Boston, MA: Pearson.

Garvis, S., Kirkby, J., McMahon, K., & Meyer, C. (2015). Collaboration is key: The actual lived experience of disciplines working together in child care. *Nursing and Health Sciences, 44*–51. doi:10.1111/nhs.12226.

Homel, R., Freiberg, K., Lamb, C., Leech, M., Carr, A., Hampshire, A., . . . Batchelor, S. (2006). *The pathways to prevention project: The first five years 1999–2004.* Brisbane: Griffith University and Mission Australia.

Kania, J., & Kramer, M. (2011). Collective impact. *Stannford Social Innovation Review,* Winter, 36–41.

Little, M., & Maughan, B. (2010). *Effective interventions for children in need.* Surrey: Ashgate.

Manning, M. (2014). Developmental interventions on children and familial wellbeing. In S. Garvis & D. Pendergast (Eds.), *Health and well-being in the early years* (pp.31–47). Cambridge: Cambridge University Press.

Manning, M., Homel, R., & Smith, C. (2010). A meta-analysis of the effects of early developmental prevention programs in at-risk populations on non-health outcomes in adolescence. *Children and Youth Services Review, 32*(4), 506–519.

Salm, T., Greenberg, H., Pitznel, M., & Cripps, D. (2010). Inter-professional education internships in schools: Jump starting change. *Journal of Inter-Professional Care, 24,* 251–263.

Tourse, R., Mooney, J. Kline, P., & Davoren, J. (2005). A collaborative model of clinical preparation: A move toward inter-professional field experience. *Journal of Social Work Education, 41,* 457–477.

Waitoller, F.R., & Kozleski, E.B. (2013).Working in boundary practices: Identity development and learning in partnerships for inclusive education. *Teaching and Teacher Education, 31*(3), 35–45.

Williams, J. (2014). Teacher educator professional learning in the third space: Implications for identity and practice. *Journal of Teacher Education, 65*(4), 315–326.

Wong, S., Sums ion, J., & Press, F. (2012). Early childhood professionals and inter-professional work in integrated early childhood services in Australia. *Australasian Journal of Early Childhood, 37*(1), 81–88.

Index

ABC Learning 3

Aboriginal people 7; *see also* Indigenous Australians

Aboriginal students 119; attendance rate of 119; issues confronting 120; *see also* Indigenous children

achievement gap 62, 73, 101, 131

agency 39, 40, 90

alcoholism *see* substance abuse

Anderson, Maybanke 12

attendance rates: in Australia 18, 56, 57, 119, 123; in Hong Kong 56; in Poland 32

Australia 1, 4, 7, 8, 17, 19, 23, 27, 34, 41, 78–80, 119, 128, 129, 148, 149; attendance rates in 18, 56, 57, 119, 123; childcare population of 38; child poverty rates in 34; compulsory education in 55–6; death rates in 95; education policy of 7, 11, 28–30, 32, 56, 120–1; giving levels of 80; life expectancy in 95–6; OECD ranking of 5, 23; paid parental leave in 23–4, 33, 146–7, 148; quality assessment 57; teacher qualifications in 56; teacher training in 45–9; universal access in 55, 56, 57

Australian Bureau of Statistics (ABS) 18, 38, 57

Australian Children's Education and Care Quality Authority (ACECQA) 19–21, 22, 45, 147

Australian Competition and Consumer Commission 3

Australian Early Development Census *see* Australian Early Development Index

Australian Early Development Index (AEDI) 4, 17, 125, 127, 128, 129

Australian Framework *see Belonging, Being and Becoming: The Early Years Learning Framework for Australia*

Australian government 2, 4, 5, 7, 8, 11, 13–14, 18, 19, 23–5, 27, 47, 80, 143, 147; 'Closing the Gap' policy 119, 120, 131, 134, 135; Department of Education and Training 28; and early childhood policy 33–4; funding of early childhood services 34; Office for Learning and Teaching 143; portfolio location of childcare policies 8, 28–30, 32, 33–4, 146

Australian Learning Framework *see Belonging, Being and Becoming: The Early Years Learning Framework for Australia*

Australian National Curriculum 50

becoming 41–2, 44

behavior: antisocial 74, 87, 91, 102; bifacial effects 98; collective 99; disorders/difficulties 128, 130; disruptive 88, 98; human 111; individual 99; management skills 94; problem 112n1; prosocial 87

behavioral paradigm 6

being 41–2, 44

belonging 41–2, 44

Belonging, Being and Becoming: The Early Years Learning Framework for Australia 15–16, 38, 41–4, 48, 56; learning outcomes of 42; *see also* becoming; being; belonging

biological embedding 90

brain plasticity 68, 71, 101; lifelong 68

Index 153

breastfeeding 24, 33
Brisbane 3
British Cohort Study 71
Broderick, Elizabeth 25
Bureau of Rural Sciences 80

Canada: giving levels of 80; Headstart
  program of 128
capability-deprivation 95
care 1; marketization of 2; *see also*
  early childhood education and care
  (ECEC)
Carolina Abecedarian Project (ABC) 69,
  72; Chapel Hill, North Carolina 69
causal pathways 75, 89–90; model 90
Certificate III level early childhood
  education and care qualification 21,
  22, 26, 27, 45, 47
Chicago Child-Parent Centre 65, 72
childcare 1–4, 12–14, 22, 25, 27, 28,
  31, 38–9, 47, 48, 49, 71, 72, 98, 130;
  after-school care 38; before-school care
  38; family day care 21, 26, 38, 136n1;
  formal 38–9, 57; in Hong Kong 54;
  informal 38–9, 57; and grandparents
  38–9, 57; *see also* early childhood
  education and care; long day care
Child Care Act 1
Child Care Benefit (CCB) 14;
  Grandparent Child Care Benefit
  (GCCB) 14; Special Child Care
  Benefit (SCCB) 14
Child Care Rebate (CCR) 14; *see also*
  Child Care Benefit (CCB)
childcare services 3, 12–13, 28, 130
childcare teachers: professional
  status of 22; salary of 22; *see also*
  teacher education/training; teacher
  qualifications
child-parent attachment 93, 111
child poverty 5, 31–3, 34, 147; *see also*
  poverty
children: agency of 39–41, 56; at-risk
  74; of culturally and linguistically
  diverse (CALD) backgrounds 122;
  with disabilities 122; disadvantaged
  3, 68, 73, 88, 101–2, 109, 125, 129,
  133, 145; images of 40; mainstream
  Australian 74, 119–36; as parental
  choice 31; parental responsibility
  for 32; wellbeing of 44, 145; *see also*
  vulnerable children

children's learning 15, 19, 26–7,
  39–45, 50, 55–7, 100, 142;
  collaborative 40, 45; community as
  site of 39–40; cultural context in 40,
  43; family as site of 39–40; formalised
  50; intentional 44; and leisure 45;
  and meaning-making 39, 40, 48;
  participatory 39, 42; play-based 41,
  43, 45, 50; spiritual dimension of
  43–4, 57; *see also* play
children's rights 18, 56; discourse 39
child-to-educator ratios 3, 19, 21, 27, 55
chronosystem 99
citizenship 12, 26, 41, 45, 63
collective impact initiatives 145
Commonwealth Department of
  Families, Housing, Community
  Services and Indigenous Affairs 80
Commonwealth Government 4, 15
Commonwealth Scientific and Industrial
  Research Organisation 80
communities 4, 13, 15–17, 19, 33–4,
  39–40, 42, 44, 69, 79, 89, 98, 100,
  120–5, 128, 134–5, 145–6, 148;
  disadvantaged 125, 145–6; Indigenous
  124–5, 128, 135, 148; mainstream 98,
  144–5; marginalized 98, 144–5; remote
  17, 120, 123, 128, 134–5; at-risk 69;
  socially disadvantaged 145, 146
Communities That Care (CTC) 144–5,
  146; *see also* interdisciplinary ways of
  working
compulsory schooling/education 2, 15,
  54–6
corporate social responsibility 79
Council of Australian Governments
  (COAG) 4, 15, 18, 43, 119
crime 65, 72, 73, 76, 88, 93, 102,
  119–20
cultural- historical paradigm 6
Cultural Revolution 68; and "sent-down
  generation" 68

day nurseries *see* childcare services
delinquency 87, 91, 93, 98, 111
Denmark 23
developmental intervention 89, 91; *see
  also* early intervention
developmental lifecourse (DLC) theory:
  perspective 7, 87–9, 111–12, 142,
  144; prevention 101; principles
  of 93–5

developmental paradigm 6
developmental pathways model
90, 112n1
developmental prevention 7, 87, 89–90,
94, 100, 144–5, 146; centre-based
developmental day care 102; enriched
preschool programs 102; family-based
102; home-visitation 102; parenting
programs 102; structured preschool
programs 102, 109
developmental systems theory 98, 100,
112n2, 145
deviance 87, 88, 102; social 109, 129
diploma-level early childhood
qualification 21, 22, 26, 45, 47
diversity 18, 40, 43, 57, 78, 125;
cultural 44, 50; religious 44
domestic violence 94, 99, 119–20
drug abuse *see* substance abuse

early childhood development *see* early
childhood education and care
early childhood education and care
(ECEC) 11, 15; access to 124,
128, 131, 135, 147; assistance
for in Australia 13–14; children
participating in 121–5, 127–32;
cost of 13–14, 27, 31, 132, 135,
147; cost-effectiveness of 135,
148; cultural responsiveness of
135; economic benefits/return
on investment of 64–5, 68, 72–4,
75–6, 102, 147, 148; educators for
132–3; future of in Australia 141–2,
146, 149; and health provision 134;
learning frameworks for 43–4; market
services model of 4; mobile services
128; nannies in 27–8; and parental
trust in 124; and 'participatory'
involvement 39; policy in Australia
11, 13, 28, 33, 120, 128, 146; as
private good 32; private sector in
Australia 23, 32–3; as public good
5, 23, 33; qualification fees for 22;
quality of 15, 120, 132, 135; right to
18; sector 8; targeted 133; universal
133, 146; *see also* Indigenous children
early childhood education policy *see*
early childhood education and care
(ECEC)

early childhood educators 41–4, 87;
marginalization of 143; qualifications
of 19, 21, 26–7
early childhood sector 8, 9, 27, 27, 33,
44, 51, 53, 142, 149; care vs. education
debate 11; privatization of 1–2
early development interventions *see* early
intervention
early intervention 2, 7, 16, 87, 89,
90–3, 100, 101, 112, 147; benefits of
71–3, 101–2; indicated 91; intensity
of 109–10; length of 109–10; risk-
focused approach of 102; targeted 91;
universal 91; *see also* outcomes
early learning *see* early childhood
education and care
early years learning framework 18; *see
also Belonging, Being and Becoming:
The Early Years Learning Framework
for Australia*
ecological theory 98, 112n2, 145
economics perspective 7, 62–82, 142
education: and health 68–71, 143, 147;
right to 33, 41
educational change model 51–4, 56,
147–8; myths about 52
educational gap 119–36
educational outcomes 87, 88, 90, 102,
109–10, 112, 125, 129, 131
educational support programs 93;
effect on behavioral and academic
problems 93
education perspective 7, 38–57, 142
Ellis, Kate 28
Elmira Nurse Home Visitation Program 76
employment outcomes 71, 73, 81,
88, 119
England 95
equity 40, 42, 50; of access 13
Europe 18, 23; countries of 18, 19
European Union (EU) 30–1;
employment rate in 30–1
exosystem 98

Fairer Paid Parental Leave Bill 2015
24–5
falsifiability 110–11, 112
Families as First Teachers (FaFT)
program 134
father(s) 24; parental leave for 30–1;
role of 24

Index 155

Fetal Alcohol Spectrum Disorder (FASD) 91–2; alcohol-related birth defects (ARBD) 92; alcohol-related neuro-developmental disorders (ARND) 92–3; fetal alcohol syndrome (FAS) 92; partial fetal alcohol syndrome (FAS) 92
foster care 64
France 23
functional capabilities 87, 94–5, 98

Gillard, Julia 28
Good Start 3
grade retention 63
Groves, Eddy 3

health outcomes 7, 62, 68, 74, 81, 88, 90, 101–2, 112, 129
Heckman, James 2, 66, 73–6, 82, 101, 102
HighScope Perry Preschool program 64–5, 72, 75–6, 82
Home Interaction Program for Parents and Youngsters (HIPPY) 134
Hong Kong: attendance rates in 56, 57; childcare centers in 54; *Children First, Right Start for All* 54–5; compulsory education in 55–6; cram schools in 54; early childhood education in 7, 38, 54–6; Education Bureau 55; education policy in 56; elitism in 54; *Guide to the Pre-Primary Curriculum* 55; kindergartens in 54–5; performance indicators in 55; preschool in 54; quality assessment 57; teacher qualifications in 56; teacher-to-children ratios in 55; tutors in 54; and universal access 55, 56, 57
Howard government 2, 28
human capital 4, 7, 63, 68, 74, 77–82; investment in 74, 75, 77–8, 79–80, 82; philanthropy 80–1; theory 63–4, 68
Human Rights Commission 25

Iceland 23; infant/toddler programs in 48
identity 16, 42, 54, 111; and relationships 41; as socioculturally constructed 40
immigrant children: experiences of 50–1

Indigenous Australians 119–20, 121, 148; culture 124, 127–8, 130, 135; diversity among 125; languages of 125; mental wellbeing of 128; outcomes for 119; quality of life of 120; *see also* Indigenous children
Indigenous children 18, 119–36, 129; 'Closing the Gap' target 120, 131, 134–5; cognitive outcomes 129–30, 135; developmental outcomes 129–31, 135; developmental vulnerability of 134; educational gap 119, 134–5; health inequalities of 134; participation in ECEC 121–4, 125, 127–32, 135; school readiness of 134; and standardized testing 125, 130
inequality 73; economic 65, 81; gender 149; social 65
intentional teaching 40, 43, 44
interdisciplinary approach 141–9; *see also* interdisciplinary ways of working "Interdisciplinary Education for the Early Years" 143–4; national interdisciplinary learning and teaching framework 143–4; *see also* interdisciplinary ways of working
interdisciplinary perspective 8
interdisciplinary ways of working 2, 8, 141–6, 147, 149; and boundary practices 142; in education 142–3; in health care 142; internationally 148–9; and inter-professional training 143; studies of 143–6
Israel 23

Jamaica 73, 101–2
Jobs, Education and Training Child Care Fee Assistance (JETCCFA) 14; *see also* Child Care Benefit (CCB)

kindergarten 11–13, 21, 48, 54–5, 89, 101, 109, 125, 136n1; and middle-class norms 12; pre- 72
Kindergarten Union 12

language acquisition 17, 41, 55, 69, 93, 94, 101, 127
learning environment 27, 33, 43, 87, 89, 133; collaborative 40
Liberal Party (Australia) 24
life expectancy 95–7

156 Index

lifelong learning 51, 55
literacy 41, 50, 94, 119, 125, 129, 130
long day care 3, 21–2, 26, 38, 47, 136n1, 144
Longitudinal Study of Indigenous Children (LSIC) 120–1, 123, 125, 129
Luxembourg 23

macrosystem 99
Maori students 124
maternity leave *see* paid parental leave
maturational paradigm 6
Melbourne Declaration on Education Goals for Young Australians 41
mental health screening 64
mental illness 99
mesosystem 98
microsystem 98
mortality rates 95, 97
mother(s) 11–12, 63, 76, 82n2; disadvantaged 11, 81; first-time 72, 91; Indigenous 124; parental leave for 24, 30, 32; working 12, 25, 30–1; *see also* breastfeeding
motherhood 13
multiculturalism 50
MyChild website (mychild.gov.au) 19, 20
MySchool website 20
My time, our place Framework for School Age Care in Australia 44–5

nannies 27–8
National Disability Strategy 16
National Early Childhood Development Strategy 4, 15, 26
National Framework for Protecting Australia's Children, 'Protecting Children is Everyone's Business' 16
National Framework for Universal Child and Family Health Services 16–17
National Health and Hospital Reform Report 16
National Partnership Agreement on Universal Access to Early Childhood Education 17–18, 23; government funding 23
National Quality Framework (NQF) for Early Childhood Education and Care 4, 5, 15, 21, 27, 47, 120, 132, 135, 136n1
National Quality Standards (NQS) 5, 15, 19

neural sculpting 90
neurogenesis 71
'new social studies of childhood' 39
New South Wales 3, 12, 21, 123; public schools 49
New Zealand 78, 124; paid parental leave 24
Northern territory 134
Norway 18; infant/toddler programs in 48
numeracy 41, 50, 119, 130
Nurse Family Partnership Program 72

Organisation for Economic Co-operation and Development (OECD) 34; countries of 5, 23, 24; indicators 5
outcomes 149; behavioral 24, 120, 129–30; cognitive development 88, 102, 109–10, 129, 135; criminal justice involvement 64–5, 74, 88, 91, 102, 109, 121, 129; developmental 63, 87, 98, 130–1, 135, 136n1, 146; economic 25, 112; familial wellbeing 102, 109–10, 129; learning 42–3, 56, 131; psychological 112; social deviance 102, 109, 129; social-emotional development 41, 45, 55, 81, 88, 99, 102, 109–10, 112, 129; social participation 88, 102, 109; *see also* educational outcomes; employment outcomes; health outcomes

Papua New Guinea 23
parental abuse and neglect 93, 101, 119
parental leave 7, 11, 146–7; paid 23–5, 30–3, 148
paternal bonds 24
Pathways to Prevention Program 144–5; *see also* interdisciplinary ways of working
peer influence 93
philanthropy 79–81
Philanthropy Australia 79, 80
play 45, 69; children's right to 41; in learning 22, 41, 43, 45, 50, 89
Poland: Big Family Card 32; child poverty rates in 31–2; education policy of 7, 32; health care in 32; parental leave in 32; preschool in 32; tax relief in 32
political perspective 7

positivist paradigm 6
postmodern paradigm 6, 39–40
poststructural paradigm 6, 39–40, 42
poverty 11, 12, 34, 81, 95, 98, 99, 149;
  child 5, 31, 33, 34, 62, 147
Prenatal and Early Childhood Nurse
  Home Visitation Program 74, 91
private equity investment 78
Productivity Commission 25–7, 121
protective factor(s) 87, 89, 91, 93–4, 111
proximal processes 98

quality of life 63, 88, 95, 97–8, 100,
  121, 146; definition 94
Queensland 46, 143

responsible investment 78–9
Responsible Investment Association
  Australasia 78–9
risk factor(s) 69, 91, 93; fixed 93;
  variable 93
Rudd government: first 28
Russia 23

school-age care 44–5
school drop-out 88, 91; rates 131
'schoolification' 26, 49–50, 56; see also
  transition to schooling
school readiness 49–50, 62, 89–90,
  120, 124–5, 128, 132, 134
Slovenia 18, 23
social good 78
socialisation process 26, 50, 93
social justice 2, 40, 64
social science research conditions
  110–11, 135; see also falsifiability
socio-behaviourist theories 42
socio-cultural paradigm 6, 39, 40, 42
Spain 23
special education placement 63
substance abuse 82n2, 93, 99, 102,
  119–20
superannuation funds 78–9
Sweden: child allowance in 31; child
  poverty rates in 31; early childhood
  services in 34; education policy of 7,
  11, 18, 30–1; employment rate in
  30–1; gender pay gap in 31; health
  care in 31; infant/toddler programs
  48; parental leave in 30; pregnancy

benefits in 31; preschool in 31;
  Stockholm 31

Tasmania 21, 46
teacher education/training 7, 12,
  38, 45–9, 56, 147; infant/toddler
  practicum 47–9
teacher qualifications 7, 22, 27, 33, 56,
  133, 149; bachelor degree 47–8; and
  ECEC quality 133; master degree
  46–8; practicum and professional
  experience 45–7; and student test
  scores 133; see also Certificate III
  level early childhood education and
  care qualification; diploma-level
  early childhood qualification; teacher
  education/training
Teachers' Association 13
teenage pregnancy 102
Torres Strait Islander students 119;
  attendance rate of 119; issues
  confronting 120; see also Indigenous
  children
toxic developmental settings 100; effect
  on schools 100
transition to schooling 15, 30, 43,
  47–50, 64, 87, 88–9, 100, 142

United Kingdom: giving levels of 80
United Nations 23; Convention on
  the Elimination of All Forms of
  Discrimination Against Women 23;
  Convention on the Rights of the
  Child 18–19, 39, 41; Principles of
  Responsible Investment 78
United States: early childhood interventions
  in 71–2; home visiting programs 73,
  101–2; infant/toddler programs in 48;
  paid parental leave in 23–4
universal access 5, 17–18, 33, 55–7,
  149; agreements 8, 47, 146
universal health services 4, 15, 16

Victoria 21, 51
vulnerable children 4, 13, 15, 18, 88,
  91, 93, 98, 100, 112, 127–9, 145

Wales 95
Western Australia 46, 128, 143
World Health Organisation 24